Antibodies, anarchangels and other essays

Paul Cudenec

Published by Winter Oak Press, Sussex, England

winteroak@greenmail.net

ISBN: 978-0-9576566-1-1

CONTENTS

PAUL CUDENEC

INTRODUCTION

Welcome to this new collection of essays featuring some of my writing dating from 2004 to 2013. Although this book is being published after *The Anarchist Revelation*, which is also on the Winter Oak imprint, most of the material here obviously predates that work.

The first and longest essay is *Antibodies: Life, Death and Resistance in the Psyche of the Superorganism*, which I wrote in 2010 and brought out as a limited-run A4 booklet.

A short note on the inside cover of that version declared that its message had emerged "from a lifetime of gnawing political, environmental and existential despair and a strong urge to somehow make sense of it all".

That could be true of anything I've written, to be honest. I have been searching for connections and parallels that might help me, and others, understand what our existence is all about. That process will never be complete and so anything committed to paper can only ever offer a partial explanation.

Antibodies is an attempt to bring together a wide range of apparently quite separate ideas into one argument. It touches on all sorts of areas that merit further investigation and which I will hopefully find the time to explore in more detail in the future.

Rupert Sheldrake's theories about what appears to be a

kind of "ESP", and his suggestions about the existence of "morphic fields" are fascinating, for instance. They may seem a million miles away from any sort of political discussion but, to me, the connection with anarchism is clear. We insist that the state is unnecessary and destructive because human societies can flourish by themselves. We argue that human societies can flourish by themselves because people are naturally motivated by feelings of co-operation, of solidarity and mutual aid – indeed, as Kropotkin showed, this is a prevalent theme throughout nature. The need and ability for close co-operation is such that groups of animals, including humans, can be seen to be acting as essentially one entity which happens to be divided into physically separate units, for the sake of convenience. Sheldrake's findings on currently inexplicable mental links between humans and animals are a bridge to the further level of understanding that life on Earth, or Gaia, is an interconnected, living, Whole and not a spherical battleground of rival individual creatures engaged in the mythical right-wing neo-Darwinist "struggle for survival".

We can then take that theme a step further by suggesting that the whole cosmos is in fact one organic entity – an idea backed up by contemporary science. Here we find that the path of our enquiry has led us to the very edge of religious belief, from which most anarchists run a mile! But there's no need, as this holistic concept is in fact eminently compatible with anarchism, which is founded on ideas of communalities that transcend the usual borders, of universality and of the natural law of mutual aid that binds us to the rest of humankind and to the world (indeed universe) in which we live.

Antibodies – which goes on to discuss the role which individuals can and must play in ensuring that we are able to live in the way we should live – is necessarily a sketch of this vision and I am aware that it skims very rapidly over subject matters that no doubt deserve weightier consideration. It would be encouraging to think that other anarchists might feel inspired to fill in one or two of the many gaps I have left!

We Anarchangels of Creative Destruction is a shorter piece of writing, which I distributed as a free A5 pamphlet in 2011. Here I experimented with a slightly different way of writing. In the foreword I explain that the text itself came to me in a dream, for which the reader will have to allow me some poetic licence. It is true, however, that the flow of the argument was such that I felt I could not convey it by means of the usual style of using quotations as part of the argument. Instead I relegated them to the endnotes. Part of this was pragmatic – the careful arguments expounded by René Guénon, for instance, are not easily broken down into snappy phrases and would have cluttered up the body of the main text. But there was also a desire on my part to express myself with a little more passion than is allowed by the academic style of writing – after all, my main purpose is to convey ideas and opinion rather than to dissect them in a dry and purportedly objective fashion.

I'm not sure what others felt about this formula, but I considered it a success on its own terms. I continued in the same vein in a creative piece called *The Task* and later set out when writing *The Anarchist Revelation* to combine this slightly more poetic writing style with a certain academic rigour.

At first glance, *The Politics of Fear: Terrorism and State Control* may not seem to fit in too well with the other writing here. This is an updated version of something I wrote in 2008, explaining how the US and UK have secretly used terrorism in Europe (as well as elsewhere) to further their political aims, specifically through the Gladio network. It is based on the books and TV documentary listed in the endnotes, but I have not provided specific references in the way I would have done today.

We are including it here because it helps to explain the background to my statements elsewhere about the complete lack of democracy in our society, about the way any social evolution away from environmental destruction and capitalist greed is blocked by those forces with a vested interest in maintaining the status quo. It helps to explain why I insist that we don't live in a democracy but in a tyranny that pretends it's a democracy in order to keep the population pacified and under control. As I write in the essay: "If this system is ruthless enough to commit acts of terrorism on its own public, or stage *coups d'état* to preserve its total grip on power, can anyone really believe it would allow a radical group to take that power away from it by winning an election?"

The most fundamental blockages to the life-force of humankind lie at a deeper level than these issues around political repression, but understanding them is a necessary stepping stone towards seeing the whole picture. The idea that the dominant system represents "security", "democracy" and "decency" is one of the most significant veils hiding the unspeakable truth of its real nature. If this veil can be removed, it will help people to be able to make out that much more clearly the shape of the monster which ultimately lies behind all the layers of disguise – a monster with no heart, no soul and no compassion which will eventually devour and destroy us all and everything that makes our lives worth living in order to satiate its own lust for ever-increasing power and wealth.

With this in mind, I find it disturbing that, although the facts about Gladio have been available for many years now, I hardly ever meet anyone who is familiar with them, even individuals with a keen interest in the manipulative ways of the state. When Allan Francovich's documentary was screened on TV in 1992, the reviewer in *The Times* commented that its incredibly significant revelations seemed to have barely registered on the news agenda of the day, and there remains a strange silence around the whole issue. I know that anarchists, and others, are often wary about wading into "conspiracy theory" territory, not wanting to be sucked into association with insane or toxic theories founded on little more than paranoia (or perhaps an agenda to confuse and discredit?). But the Gladio conspiracy is not theory at all, it's fact – and it's something about which people should become informed.

The short piece called *Li and the Organic Freedom of Anarchy*, which first appeared on my blog, is very much a continuation of the theme of *Antibodies,* but with more specific reference to Taoism. The "natural order, an innate and organic pattern to life that emerges without external control or direction" is not just *li* but also anarchy.

Transcendent Anarchy invokes what I see as the strong Jungian link to anarchism, via the work of June Singer. The neurosis of the individual and the neurosis of society run parallel on their different planes, as microcosm and macrocosm: "When the natural self-correcting processes of society are blocked – by all the levels of repression and control that protect the status quo – then a neurosis develops as an 'an effort to find a way over or around the obstruction'".

Fighting Capitalism On Every Level is very much a political argument, rather than a philosophical one, although still an attempt to move people's minds out of the metaphorical rut in which they often seem stuck. The unimaginative "either/or" mentality is the bane of creative political thinking, as it leads to further assumptions that one approach is "right" and the other "wrong". It is quite possible to be convinced that you are in the right and yet still allow for the fact that comrades' views and approaches have validity. Anarchism, for me, has always been a movement or philosophy which is able to embrace and contain diversity and contradiction – indeed, that has been its greatest strength. Any attempts to control or reduce its life-affirming vigour are, fortunately, doomed to failure!

Towards the End of the Week: The Tyranny of Time first appeared in *Green Anarchist* in 2004 and was kindly saved from oblivion by the online *Anarchist Library*. It's a fairly light-hearted piece, built around the pun in the title, but apart from biblical authority, I am still to be convinced of any arguable basis for the seven-day cycle that so dominates most people's lives.

My brief dictionary definition of *Plutofascism* is self-explanatory – I do feel this is a word which perfectly describes the system under which we are now living.

We decided to include the *Interview with Paul Cudenec* which first appeared online in July 2013, as it sets out nicely my views on certain important issues, notably the relationship between anarchism and spirituality. Thanks to *The Vast Minority* (vastminority.blogspot.com) for letting us use it.

This collection concludes on a more personal note with *Don't Kill Yourself: A Letter to An Anarchist Friend*. There's a happy ending to the background story, as the comrade in question later made it clear that their thoughts of self-destruction were fleeting and there was, in fact, no need at all for me to have gone to such lengths in setting out the case for them to stay alive!

Paul Cudenec, 2013

ANTIBODIES: LIFE, DEATH AND RESISTANCE IN THE PSYCHE OF THE SUPERORGANISM

"Words do not express thoughts very well. They always become a little different immediately they are expressed, a little distorted, a little foolish. And yet it also pleases me and seems right that what is of value and wisdom to one man seems nonsense to another".

Hermann Hesse[1]

The starting point of this journey of ideas is the concept of the superorganism. It's a strange word and one that throws into question a lot of our assumptions about how life works.

An organism, a creature, seems to have quite distinct physical boundaries. It sticks together in a definite lump and is surrounded by some kind of empty space that separates it from other organisms, whether similar or dissimilar. But the idea of a superorganism, an animal that consists of parts that aren't even physically connected, opens up a lot of intriguing possibilities.

In his 1937 book *The Soul of the White Ant*, South African biologist Eugène Marais reveals that his painstaking research has convinced him that a termitary, a community of termites, in fact amounts to one collectively-formed being. He writes:

"You must consider a termitary as a single animal, whose organs have not yet been fused together as in a human being. Some of the termites form the mouth and digestive system; others take the place of weapons of defence like claws or horns; others form the generative organs".[2] He adds: "The insects themselves should always be thought of as the blood-stream and organs of a single animal".[3]

And Marais sees evidence of the same phenomenon elsewhere in the natural world. For instance, describing marine creatures called Siphonophora, he explains: "The great peculiarity of these creatures is that every full-grown specimen is a composite animal composed of hundreds of individuals".[4] Still more peculiar is Marais's suggestion that individual mammals are, in fact, examples of collective entities. He writes: "The body of a mammal with its many vital organs can be looked upon as a community with specialized individuals grouped into organs, the whole community forming the composite animal".[5]

Some 70 years later, ideas challenging traditional concepts of where an individual animal begins and ends are now interesting a new generation of biologists, not least the researcher and author Rupert Sheldrake. He writes: "We know animals have social groups, and that somehow the group as a whole is linked together so that it can function as if it were a superorganism... This is most clearly the case in the social insects, like the ants, termites, bees and wasps. It is plainly visible in a flock of birds turning and banking practically simultaneously, with none of them bumping into each other. And so it is with a school of fish swimming in close formation, but changing direction at any time, and responding rapidly to the approach of a predator".[6]

So the arguments for the existence of superorganisms depend on the way animals behave, the extent to which they work together collectively rather than individually, and the efficiency with which they do so. This was an area of intense research for another celebrated scientist, who also made a name for himself as a classical anarchist theorist. Peter Kropotkin's seminal work *Mutual Aid* (first published in 1902) describes the benefits of collective behaviour across many species. He writes: "Life in societies is no exception in the animal world; it is the rule, the law of Nature, and it reaches its fullest development with the higher vertebrates. Those species which live solitary, or in small families only, are relatively few, and their numbers are limited. Nay, it appears very probable that, apart from a few exceptions, those birds and mammals which are not gregarious now, were living in societies before man multiplied on the earth and waged a permanent war against them, or destroyed the sources from which they formerly derived food".[7]

Taking a stance against the right-wing neo-Darwinist theories current at the time – which assumed a permanent Hobbesian war for survival within nature – Kropotkin maintains that the real "struggle for life" on the planet is not between competing individuals but rather against adversity, and in this battle the key weapon is co-operation. He writes: "Even such harsh animals as the rats, which continually fight in our cellars, are sufficiently intelligent not to quarrel when they plunder our larders, but to aid one another in their plundering expeditions and migrations, and even to feed their invalids".[8] And he explains: "'Don't compete! – competition is always injurious to the species and you have plenty of resources to avoid it!' That is the tendency of nature, not always realized in full, but always present. That is the watchword that comes to us from the bush, the forest and the ocean. 'Therefore combine – practise mutual aid! That is the surest means for giving to each and to all the greatest safety, the best guarantee of existence and progress, bodily, intellectual and moral'. That is what Nature teaches us; and that is what all those animals which have attained the highest position in their respective classes have done".[9]

A similar line was taken more recently by British scientist Kit Pedler. In a book first published in 1979, he echoes Marais by comparing the communication and interaction between living creatures to that between the cells, organs and systems of a human body. Says Pedler: "In the body, for example, each organ has a particular function within the whole. The kidney has the function of removing waste from the blood, and it is supported by the physiological activities of the rest of the body. It is not, in the absence of disease, attacked by the other body systems, it is supplied with a suitable milieu for its function. Similarly, in the ecosphere, the species to some extent protect each other by creating mutually suitable conditions. Obviously, there is competition and predation as well, but mutual aid and mutual provision underlies the whole".[10]

Although, in making his case for natural solidarity, Kropotkin includes mention of the behaviour of the very ants and termites that so intrigued Marais, he certainly does not regard them as representing the epitome of this phenomenon. He does not see the instinctive collective behaviour of such insects as that of lesser beings, something likely to be left behind in the evolution of more complex or individually "intelligent" animals. He argues: "As to the intellectual faculty, while every Darwinist will agree with Darwin that it is the most powerful arm in the struggle for life, and the most powerful factor of further evolution, he also will admit that intelligence is an eminently social faculty. Language, imitation, and accumulated experience are so many elements of growing intelligence of which the unsociable animal is deprived. Therefore we find, at the top of each class of animals, the ants, the parrots and the monkeys, all combining the greatest sociability with the highest development of intelligence. The fittest are thus the most sociable animals, and sociability appears as the chief factor of evolution, both directly, by securing the well-being of the species while diminishing the waste of energy, and indirectly, by favouring the growth of intelligence".[11]

Having established the importance of mutual aid among other animals, it is but a short step to apply it to human behaviour. Kropotkin tells us: "Sociability and need of mutual aid and support are such inherent parts of human nature that at no time of history can we discover men living in small isolated families, fighting each other for the means of subsistence".[12] He continues: "The mutual-aid tendency in man has so remote an origin, and is so deeply interwoven with all the past evolution of the human race, that it has been maintained by mankind up to the present time, notwithstanding all vicissitudes of history".[13]

Of course, Kropotkin's "present time" was not quite ours and we may well argue that there is sadly little evidence of a mutual-aid mentality in the consumer societies of the wealthier parts of the modern world. But his argument is essentially that such atomisation represents a departure from the norm, rather than humanity's natural state of affairs, and he cites primitive ways of life to illustrate the underlying pattern of collective behaviour. For example, he mentions: "If anything is given to a Hottentot, he at once divides it among all present – a habit which, as is known, so much struck Darwin among the Fuegians. He cannot eat alone, and, however hungry, he calls those who pass by to share his food".[14] And he adds: "When first meeting with primitive races, the Europeans usually make a caricature of their life; but when an intelligent man has stayed among them for a longer time, he generally describes them as the 'kindest' or 'the gentlest' race on the earth. These very same words have been applied to the Ostyaks, the Samoyedes, the Eskimos, the Dayaks, the Aleoutes, the Papuas, and so on, by the highest authorities. I also remember having read them applied to the Tunguses, the Tchuktchis, the Sioux, and several others. The very frequency of that high commendation already speaks volumes in itself".[15]

Lest he be accused of romanticising primitive peoples,

Kropotkin explains: "The savage is not an ideal of virtue, nor is he an ideal of 'savagery'. But the primitive man has one quality, elaborated and maintained by the very necessities of his hard struggle for life – he identifies his own existence with that of his tribe; and without that quality mankind never would have attained the level it has attained now".[16]

The idea of what is "natural to humanity" perhaps seems rather remote and abstract, particularly when we are talking about people whose lifestyles are so very different from our own. It almost seems as if we are contemplating some worthy and elevated state of existence to which we can aspire but which in truth we will never get round to making a reality. But if we take away the anthropological slant, we can see that the general propensity still forms an important part of our everyday lives, even if it has been much reduced in contemporary society.

All we are really talking about, in essence, is socialising – having friends, neighbours, sporting team-mates and so on. We are also talking about that elusive feeling of belonging that we all value. It's nice to walk down the street where we live and be greeted by people we know. It's good to wander into a pub and have a chat with other regulars. It's enjoyable to spend time with friends. It is not hard work, not some kind of altruistic self-sacrifice, but what most of us like doing. This is what Kropotkin is referring to when he notes that it is "extremely difficult to say what brings animals together – the needs of mutual protection, or simply the pleasure of feeling surrounded by their congeners".[17]

So, to recap, the idea of a superorganism is that individuals are merely parts of a larger entity. Meanwhile, the idea of mutual aid is that a tendency to co-operation is deeply rooted in nature, including humanity. These concepts are obviously closely intertwined – a profound and innate sense of solidarity is exactly what we would expect to find if an animal group or human community were in fact functioning as a biological superorganism. And, in the knowledge that this phenomenon is universal, we might expand the theory still further to include larger groupings and eventually postulate a superorganism that embraces not just many species of animal, fish and insect, but also plants, chemicals, gases – in short, everything on the planet.

This is exactly what is meant by Gaia, a concept that has achieved widespread acceptance over the last few decades. Who better to go to for a definition than James Lovelock, the scientist who launched the idea into the public imagination? In the preface to the 2000 edition of his original 1979 book, he describes the Gaia theory as one "in which all life and all the material parts of the Earth's surface make up a single system, a kind of mega-organism, and a living planet".[18] He adds: "Gaia is the superorganism composed of all life tightly coupled with the air, the oceans, and the surface rocks".[19]

Pedler, whose exposition of the Gaia theory is more passionate and often more convincing than Lovelock's, writes that he uses the name Gaia "to encompass the idea that the entire living pelt of our planet, its thin green rind of life, is actually one single life-form with senses, intelligence and the power to act. Stretching from man to the worm, from the fishes of the abyss to the yoghurt bacterium, and from the moulds of decay to the birds riding the sky, I hold that there is but one single interwoven web of life and that our own kind was, until recently, an integral part of this single magnificent entity".[20]

This vision is not confined to the Earth, either. Pedler explicitly extends it to a universal level throughout his book and even the less holistic Lovelock concedes somewhat grudgingly that our planet is very much dependent on external factors when he notes: "Life requires a constant energy flux from the sun to sustain it".[21] So the ultimate theoretical superorganism is, in fact, the entire universe, the whole of everything. We have made a giant leap here. From the practical discussion of the habits of termites, we seem to have emerged into a positively spiritual terrain.

There is, of course, nothing new in the notion that everything in the universe is one big living entity. It may well be the oldest human concept of all, taken for granted as a fact for hundreds of thousands of years. Evidence of this primitive pantheism, the worship of nature as god, or god as nature, can be detected on every continent and in every era. Mythologist Joseph Campbell, for instance, sees its influence behind ancient cannibalistic rituals in Asia. "Psychologically," he muses, "the effect of the enactment of such a rite is to shift the focus of the mind from the individual (who perishes) to the everlasting group. Magically, it is to reinforce the ever-living life in all lives, which appears to be many but is really one".[22]

Among native Americans the universal superorganism was hailed as the Great Spirit while other cultures have attached own-brand labels to the same philosophical product. For writer Peter Marshall the key discovery is of "something all-pervasive in the universe, some invisible but palpable presence in all beings and things" and he traces a thread through Eastern religions to the medieval alchemists' belief in an *anima mundi* (world spirit).[23] Concurs Henry Margenau: "A great variety of names have described this Universal Mind, among them Tao, Logos, Brahman, Atman, the Absolute, Mana, Holy Ghost, Weltgeist or simply God". [24]

It is certainly in Eastern culture that we find contemplation of the one-ness of the universe most central to the religious viewpoint. Brahman, mentioned above, is the Hindu concept of the ultimate divine reality of the cosmos, from which all beings originate and to which they must return. Campbell describes how Japanese Buddhists believe that all beings, no matter how separate they appear, are in fact united.[25] And he defines the aim of the Amida form of Buddhism in particular as to awaken oneself to "the reality of the truth of the Flowery Wreath, that one is all and all are one".[26] Analysing the Indian tradition, he writes: "It is not that the divine is everywhere; it is that the divine is everything... It is of course true that in the popular religions of the Orient the gods are worshiped as though external to their devotees, and all the rules and rites of a covenanted relationship are observed. Nevertheless, the ultimate realization, which the sages have celebrated, is that the god worshiped as though without is in reality a reflex of the same mystery as oneself".[27]

This realization leads on to a profound spiritual experience, he explains: "One is to leap beyond God-in-the-image-of-man, man-in-the-image-of-God, and the universe cognized by the mind. The mind itself, indeed, is to break and dissolve in the burning light of a realization both above and below, beyond and yet within, everything it has conceived: an experience of the ineffable, unimaginable no-thing that is the mystery of all being and yet no mystery, since it is actually ourselves and what we are regarding every minute of the whole duration of our lives".[28]

But it would be a mistake to assume that this philosophy is confined to Eastern civilization – present in the origins of Western civilization in ancient Greece, it even surfaces from time to time in Christian thought. A prime example was the work of Meister Eckhart, the celebrated medieval mystic, who declared that "all creatures are one person, loving God by nature".[29] Expanding on the theme, he said: "The inner consciousness strikes down to the very essence of the soul. Not that it is the soul itself, but it is rooted there and is in a measure the life of the soul, her intellectual life, the life, that is, in which a man is born God's son, born into the eternal life, for this knowledge is timeless, unextended, without here and without now. In this life all things are the same thing and all things are held in common; all things are all in all, and all are one".[30]

Eckhart's understanding of God, as nothing more or less than the universe itself and lacking any moral or personal aspect, was rather at odds with the Christian norm. "It must be borne in mind that God is without will, without love, without justice, without mercy, indeed, without divinity or anything we can ascribe to him or predicate of him or attribute to him," he once argued.[31] It is perhaps not surprising that he was later excommunicated. Some 300 years later, 17th century Dutch philosopher Baruch Spinoza managed to incorporate a similar viewpoint into his unorthodox version of Christianity with his theory "that God is not distinct from the world, but immanent within it".[32] According to Roger Scruton: "Spinoza's achievement was to show man and his world as an inextricable unity, and man himself as simultaneously master and servant of the fate which creates him".[33]

The Eckhart-Spinoza version of Christianity failed to turn the religious face of the West in a more easterly and holistic direction. But that does not mean that this vision of cosmic unity, passed down from humanity's infancy and arguably embedded in our very essence, has not resurfaced in European minds time and time again. A particularly strong manifestation was in 19th and early 20th century Germany where, inspired by the greatness of Goethe, the likes of Gustav Theodor Fechner and then Wilhelm Bölsche, with his book *Das Liebleseben in der Natur* (Love in Nature), kept alive the concept of the universal psyche.[34]

The same was true of the philosopher Fritz Mauthner, whose work helped develop the *Weltanschauung* of the great German-Jewish anarchist Gustav Landauer (1870-1919). Turning Mauthner's theoretical possibility into a concrete proposition, Landauer comes to the conclusion that "the psyche [*das Seelenhafte*] in the human being is a function or manifestation of the infinite universe".[35] Landauer calls for a spiritual renewal and declares: "We must finally realize once again that we do not just perceive parts of the world but that we are ourselves parts of the world. He who could completely understand the flower would understand the universe. All right: let us return completely into ourselves, then we shall have found universe incarnate".[36] And again: "We have been satisfied until now to transform the universe into the human spirit, or better, into the human intellect; let us now transform ourselves into the universal spirit".[37] Elsewhere Landauer spells out his bold metaphysical position quite plainly: "Human beings all reach back over thousands of years as human beings, but they also existed before they were human beings, before the earth existed, back into infinity".[38]

The idea of spiritual unity with the cosmos is probably latent in any philosophy built around the embrace of nature, but it is not always explicitly expressed. One exception is the Victorian English naturalist, journalist and author Richard Jefferies, particularly in the pages of *The Story of My Heart*, first published in 1883. He tells of his desire for an enlarged "soul-life" and his conviction that "a great life – an entire civilization – lies just outside the pale of common thought". He explains: "Such life is different from any yet imagined. A nexus of ideas exists of which nothing is known – a vast system of ideas – a cosmos of thought. There is an Entity, a Soul-Entity, as yet unrecognized".[39]

Since the 1960s, this sort of thinking has been mostly associated with the New Age sub-culture, though not always voiced with the passion and clarity of Landauer or Jefferies. It also surfaces in eco-minded works of fiction such as James Cameron's film *Avatar*, in which the inhabitants of a distant planet physically plug into each other and their Earth Mother. Marshall expounds his own personal version of "a new philosophy for a new era" in a tome published at the start of the millennium: "Ultimately, holistic thinking recognizes that all things come from the One and proceed to the One. All is One and One is All. There is unity in diversity throughout the universe; indeed, the greater the diversity, the more overall the harmony. It comes as no surprise that the Greek word kosmos originally meant both the universe and harmony: they are synonymous".[40] He continues: "Ultimate Reality is the groundless ground of Being and non-Being, the primordial continuum, the mother of all. It is prior to nature and the source of all energy and life".[41]

Contemporary author Eckhart Tolle provides an interesting link between related thought systems from different eras – and not simply on the basis of his adopted forename. In his 2006 work *A New Earth*, he writes: "Since time immemorial, flowers, crystals, precious stones and birds have held special significance for the human spirit. Like all life-forms, they are, of course, temporary manifestations of the underlying one Life, one Consciousness".[42] Later in the same work, he affirms that "all things in existence, from microbes to human beings to galaxies, are not really separate things or entities, but form part of a web of interconnected multidimensional processes".[43]

The terminology in this latter quotation reflects the fact that what were once seen as hopelessly unworldly notions are now also being espoused by scientists. Scruton picks up on this while writing about Spinoza's philosophy: "There is a modern equivalent of Spinoza's monism in the view that all transformations in the world are transformations of a single stuff – matter for the Newtonians, energy for the followers of Planck and Einstein".[44] He summarises: "The individual person is not, it seems, an individual at all. Nor is anything else".[45]

Margenau defines holism as "the view that all living systems tend to form highly integrated and indivisible entities".[46] David Lorimer explains the concept in terms of forms. He says: "Forms are dynamic energy patterns whose boundaries are created by velocity. Individual self-consciousness, by analogy, might be said to arise out of unitive consciousness and erect protective barriers around itself; nevertheless, as an open system, it remains semi-permeable and can interact with other individual selves as open systems. When, however, unitive consciousness is experienced, the boundaries dissolve and there dawns the realization that one's ground is the unitive consciousness field out of which other individual self-consciousnesses also arise: the many arise out of the One and are linked to each other through participation in that One".[47]

Elucidating his own theories of connectedness, Sheldrake discusses the aspect of quantum theory called quantum "non-locality", which is also known as "non-separability" or "entanglement". He writes: "According to quantum theory, when a quantum system (such as an atom) breaks up into parts, these parts remain 'entangled' with each other in such a way that a change in one is instantaneously coupled to a change in another, even though they may be many miles apart. For example, when a pair of photons are emitted from the same atom, their polarization is undetermined, although one is obliged to have a polarization opposite to the other. As soon as the polarization of one is measured, the other has the opposite polarization instantaneously. Albert Einstein was deeply unhappy about this aspect of quantum theory precisely because it appeared to allow a 'spooky action at a distance'. But experiments have shown that quantum non-locality is indeed a fundamental feature of reality".[48]

So if all matter originally diverged from the Big Bang or whatever begun the universe, is it likewise still "entangled"? Is All really One? If so, where does this leave us, as individuals?

"If everything exists in God, in what sense does the world contain individual things, and in what sense am I an individual, with a nature and destiny which are mine?"[49] That is Scruton's *précis* of the metaphysical question posed by Spinoza in the third part of his *Ethics* and, divine reference aside, it sums up nicely the point we have now reached. Unfortunately, not all the answers provided over the centuries are entirely helpful. Eastern religions, for instance, can tell us that individuals simply do not exist and that, indeed, nothing really does at all, as we saw with Campbell's "ineffable, unimaginable no-thing" that is the ultimate purpose of a spiritual journey.

Here we will work on the assumption that we are real, and live in a real world – what we want to know is what *kind* of reality we are living. Meister Eckhart took the position that "all creatures are one person" on the basis of "the difference between the light of nature and in time and the light of that nature beyond time in eternal glory",[50] but that does not really help in practical terms. For the psychologist Carl Jung: "Man as an individual is a very suspicious phenomenon whose right to exist could be questioned by the biologist, since from that point of view he is significant only as a collective creature or as a particle in the mass".[51]

Pedler describes how his view of his own existence changed completely from the moment he realised the universe was "a swirling mass of atoms" of which we formed just a tiny part. He says: "From this time on, it has been impossible for me to maintain the idea that my skin limits my individuality. My body only allows my thoughts to move about, my hands to make things and my senses and experience to travel the planet I live on. But as I move, the matter of the universe moves through me as easily as the wind through the branches of trees".[52]

He also provides an explanation of how he thinks this might work. "And yet, you may argue, we are not a part of any other creature or entity," he concedes. "We are obviously individuals, separate from Gaia. We have individual brains which direct the activities of individual physical bodies limited by skin. Beyond the skin, there is space and then beyond the space the skin of another individual and so on. We also believe that we have choice, freewill and the capacity to act. We need to believe this view of things to get about the everyday world of tools and cities. As a hesitant Gaian, if I may coin the word, I see individuality as a temporary separation from the fabric of the universal life process. Imagine a flexible sheet of infinite extent. All plants, animals and humans emerge from the sheet as if someone had pushed a finger against the reverse side and made it bulge. The bulge becomes a sphere with a thin neck still attached. Then the neck becomes almost infinitely thin and the now individual life in the sphere is born and free for just a lifetime. At death, the sphere contracts down on to the surface of the sheet, flattens and flows out again into the whole until there is finally no trace of its previous existence. Imagine this process going on in both directions, millions and millions of times every second as the life process ebbs and flows between the separate and the conjugate. There is continuous change, motion and balance to produce stability and it is only we who imagine, falsely, that we are building a separate permanence".[53]

Margenau adopts a similar position, suggesting that "each of us is the Universal Mind but inflicted with limitations that obscure all but a tiny fraction of its aspects and properties".[54] Landauer describes the individual as "a flash within the stream of psyche, which one calls according to the context 'human race', 'species' or 'universe'". He adds that "it is time for the insight that there is no individual, but only unities and communities. It is not true that collective names designate only a sum of individuals: on the contrary, individuals are only manifestations and points of reference, electric sparks of something grand and whole".[55]

The idea that individuals do not exist is potentially quite upsetting for those of us who value our personal freedom and our ability to think for ourselves. Even the act of reading these words and pondering over the issues raised constitutes a statement of individual intent and existence. However, there is a corollary to the hypothetic non-reality of individuals that makes the whole package a more attractive proposition. Campbell recounts an anecdote about the Taoist sage Chuang Tzu, who lived around 300BC, and his cheerful reaction to his wife's death. He is said to have told people: "When she died, I was in despair, as any man well might be. But soon, pondering on what had happened, I told myself that in death no strange new fate befalls us. In the beginning we lack not life only, but form; not form only, but spirit. We are blent in the one great featureless, undistinguishable mass. Then a time came when the mass evolved spirit, spirit evolved form, form evolved life. And now life in its turn has evolved death".[56]

Eckhart makes the same point when he declares: "In my eternal mode of birth I have always been, am now, and shall eternally remain".[57] And Charles B Maurer explains how Mauthner also addresses the "interesting implications" of his theories regarding individuality and comes to the conclusion that "death becomes a relative concept, life an enduring unity"[58] and that "the death of the individual is then only a phase in the life of the organism".[59]

If individuals don't really exist in the first place, then they can never really die. As a part of the whole, as part of nature, we possess immortality if only we could see it. "A tree is an extension of the earth," states Pedler. "A tree is part of the sun, because the rays of the sun are its life. A tree does not end at its roots. It is an organ of Gaia. The tree is Gaia and Gaia is the tree. It is living earth. A man is not a man, he is an extension of the earth. A man and a woman are part of the sun because the rays of the sun are their life. A tree, a man and a woman are the same because they are an extension of the earth. When they are alive, they are together because they are the same. When they die they go on together, because they are still the same".[60]

Tolle also uses a tree, or rather a sapling that fails to grow into one, to illustrate his case. He writes: "We could say that the totality – Life – wants the sapling to become a tree, but the sapling doesn't see itself as separate from life and so wants nothing for itself. It is one with what Life wants. That's why it isn't worried or stressed. And if it has to die prematurely, it dies with ease. It is as surrendered in death as it is in life. It senses, no matter how obscurely, its rootedness in Being, the formless and eternal one Life".[61]

Jefferies experiences a mystic revelation of his immortality. "Recognizing my own inner consciousness, the psyche, so clearly, death did not seem to me to affect the personality," he writes. "In dissolution there was no bridgeless chasm, no unfathomable gulf of separation; the spirit did not immediately become inaccessible, leaping at a bound to an immeasurable distance. Look at another person while living; the soul is not visible, only the body which it animates. Therefore, merely because after death the soul is not visible is no demonstration that it does not still live. The condition of being unseen is the same condition which occurs while the body is living, so that intrinsically there is nothing exceptionable, or supernatural, in the life of the soul after death. Resting by the tumulus, the spirit of the man who had been interred there was to me really alive, and very close. This was quite natural, as natural and simple as the grass waving in the wind, the bees humming, and the larks' songs. Only by the strongest effort of the mind could I understand the idea of extinction; that was supernatural, requiring a miracle; the immortality of the soul natural, like the earth. Listening to the sighing of the grass I felt immortality as I felt the beauty of the summer morning, and I thought beyond immortality, of other conditions, more beautiful than existence, higher than immortality".[62]

Jung expresses the same feeling when he writes of the importance of psychic energy: "This is our immortality, the link through which man feels inextinguishably one with the continuity of all life. The life of the psyche is the life of mankind. Welling up from the depths of the unconscious, its springs gush forth from the root of the whole human race, since the individual is, biologically speaking, only a twig broken off from the mother and transplanted".[63]

The great Russian writer Leo Tolstoy takes a slightly different slant when he argues that there is no need for us to fear death, as we do not exist in a fixed frame of identity throughout our lives in any case. He explains: "Our body is not one, and that which recognizes this changing body to be one and ours is not continuous in point of time, but is merely a series of changing states of consciousness, and we have already lost both our body and our consciousness many times; we lose our body constantly, and we lose our consciousness every day, when we fall asleep, and every day and hour we feel in ourselves the alteration of this consciousness and we do not fear it in the least".[64] And at the same time he deploys the inevitability of death, and the shadow it can cast over life, as an argument against seeking satisfaction in one's life as an individual – a quest doomed to failure by our physical mortality. He says: "The sole aim of life, as it first presents itself to man, is the happiness of himself as an individual, but individual happiness there cannot be; if there were anything resembling individual happiness in life, then that life in which alone happiness can exist, the life of the individual, is borne irresistibly, by every movement, by every breath, towards suffering, towards evil, towards death, towards annihilation. And this is so self-evident and so plain that every thinking man, old or young, learned or unlearned, will see it".[65]

As well as shedding light on the necessary limitations of our individual physical existences, the notion of immortality within the whole can also lead us to see death as liberation. Declares Tolle: "When forms around you die or death approaches, your sense of Beingness, of I Am, is freed from its entanglement with form: Spirit is released from its imprisonment in matter. You realize your essential identity as formless, as an all-pervasive Presence, of Being prior to all forms, all identifications. You realize your true identity as consciousness itself, rather than what consciousness had identified with".[66]

Jung describes the yearning for death felt by the archetypal hero, psychologically present in us all: "Always he imagines his worst enemy in front of him, yet he carries the enemy within himself – a deadly longing for the abyss, a longing to drown in his own source, to be sucked down to the realm of the Mothers. His life is a constant struggle against extinction, a violent yet fleeting deliverance from ever-lurking night. This death is no external enemy, it is his own inner longing for the stillness and profound peace of all-knowing non-existence, for all-seeing sleep in the ocean of coming-to-be and passing away. Even in his highest strivings for harmony and balance, for the profundities of philosophy and the raptures of the artist, he seeks death, immobility, satiety, rest".[67]

Our current civilization has a strange relationship to death. While the high incidence of suicide (of both the quick and slow variety) points to a widespread longing for Jung's "profound peace", our own mortality is a reality we tend to avoid confronting. With so much of our being invested in our own specific individuality – our personal history, our personal family, our friends, our work, our possessions and so on – we find it hard to accept that it will one day surrender itself completely to the whole, like a raindrop falling into the ocean.

Our religions provide a version of death in which our precious individuality remains intact thereafter and in which we can even re-engage with other individuals to whom we have become attached during our physical lifetimes. For most people, losing their individuality on their death would amount to the same thing as being completely extinguished. What this tells us is that, even if we are all just small temporary parts of a greater unity, we are not generally aware of this and thus find it no consolation that this unity possesses an immortality in which we share. While physically it cannot be possible for us to cease to be connected to something which constitutes our very essence, mentally it would seem that we have become predominantly separated from the great one-ness of the cosmos. How exactly has this come about?

"It has taken me all of my life so far to realize that the single great obstacle in the way of survival and an extended human vision is the industrial society itself, and its expropriation and suppression of the most sensitive and creative qualities of the mind".[68] Thus writes Pedler in his inspiring evocation of the spirit of Gaia. He sees the very trappings of modern existence, from cars to washing machines, as barriers between us and our true identity with the natural whole: "They are symbols of despair and failure: surrogates for achievement, which encourage us to live on the outside of our senses and actually diminish the quality of life".[69]

American eco-philosopher John Zerzan states: "The more technicized and artificial the world becomes, and as the natural world is evacuated, there's an obvious sense of being alienated from a natural embeddedness".[70]

It hardly seems necessary to spell out the ways in which high-tech civilization contributes to our divorce from nature. Cocooned in moving steel cages and in brick or concrete prisons, barely aware of the existence of a world beyond the consumer comforts we are trained to treasure, cut off from the source of our nourishment, living our lives second-hand through manufactured images pumped into our brains to align our imagination with the demands of the vast, all-devouring machine on which we have become pathologically dependent – one would say our separation could hardly be more complete if one was not dreadfully aware of the horrors that could yet lie in store for future generations.

The Invisible Committee, authors of provocative French political pamphlet *The Coming Insurrection*, point to Reebok's "I am what I am" marketing slogan as the epitome of this malaise. It is, they say, "not simply a lie, a simple advertising campaign, but a military campaign, a war cry directed against everything that exists between beings, against everything that circulates indistinctly, everything that invisibly links them, everything that prevents complete desolation, against everything that makes us exist, and ensures that the whole world doesn't everywhere have the look and feel of a highway, an amusement park or a new town: pure boredom, passionless but well-ordered empty, frozen space, where nothing moves apart from registered bodies, molecular automobiles and ideal commodities".[71] However, this process did not begin with the internet or the mobile phone and what we are experiencing now is the culmination of many years of progressive deterioration and separation.

A century ago, for instance, Landauer was aware of the way industrial society was destroying the collective spirit, or *Geist*, that connects us to the whole. "The most obvious sign of the absence of *Geist* was for Landauer the plight of the industrial workers. Separated from the earth and its products and spiritually isolated from each other despite the closeness of their living conditions, they become victims of alcohol, disease, and poverty. The relationship between worker and employer becomes completely dehumanized through capitalism, technology, and the state".[72] Comments Zerzan: "Science, the model of progress, has imprisoned and interrogated nature, while technology has sentenced it (and humanity) to forced labor. From the original dividing of the self that is civilization, to Descartes' splitting of the mind from the rest of objects (including the body), to our arid, high-tech present – a movement indeed wondrous".[73]

For some thinkers, the passing of the Middle Ages represented an ominous step towards the abyss for western civilization. Writes Maurer: "Landauer viewed the development of individualism, one of the most significant features of the Renaissance, as a factor that ran counter to *Geist* and undermined its hold upon medieval life... Since that time Europe has been involved in a constant struggle to reattain a level of stability such as marked the Middle Ages. This struggle is a long-lasting revolution against dogmatism for the reestablishment of *Geist* as the fundamental principle of human life".[74] Kropotkin shares this view. He explains: "The mediaeval cities were not organized upon some preconceived plan in obedience to the will of an outside legislator. Each of them was a natural growth in the full sense of the word – an always varying result of struggle between various forces which adjusted and re-adjusted themselves in conformity with their relative energies, the chances of their conflicts, and the support they found in their surroundings".[75]

He says of the medieval guild: "It had its own self-jurisdiction, its own military force, its own general assemblies, its own traditions of struggles, glory, and independence, its own relations with other guilds of the same trade in other cities: it had, in a word, a full organic life which could only result from the integrality of the vital functions".[76] With the end of the medieval federations, he says, came the start of the central state – the rule of a despot supposedly acting "in the interests of" the people. "And, with this new direction of mind and this new belief in one man's power, the old federalist principle faded away, and the very creative genius of the masses died out".[77] He adds: "The absorption of all social functions by the State necessarily favoured the development of an unbridled narrow-minded individualism. In proportion as the obligations towards the State grew in numbers the citizens were evidently relieved from their obligations towards each other".[78]

So the tyranny of central control, of the state, destroys the living superorganism of a healthy human society. It cuts out the connections between individuals and extinguishes the collective spirit, the *Geist*, which binds them together and enables them to function as nature intended. Perhaps more surprisingly, Kropotkin also identifies the family unit as contributing to the gradual process of separation and alienation. He writes: "Far from being a primitive form of organization, the family is a very late product of human evolution. As far as we can go back in the palaeo-ethnology of mankind, we find men living in societies – in tribes similar to those of the higher mammals; and an extremely slow and long evolution was required to bring these societies to the gentile, or clan organization, which, in its turn, had to undergo another, also very long evolution, before the first germs of family, polygamous or monogamous, could appear. Societies, bands or tribes – not families – were thus the primitive form of organization of mankind and its earliest ancestors".[79]

He describes the negative effect of this break-down of communal life at a stage when "the separate patriarchal family had slowly but steadily developed within the clans, and in the long run it evidently meant the individual accumulation of wealth and power, and the hereditary transmission of both".[80]

Others look to the field of religion for clues as to how humanity's separation from nature, indeed from its very own nature, occurred. Campbell pinpoints the difference between Eastern and Western creation myths: "In the Indian version it is the god himself that divides and becomes not man alone but all creation; so that everything is a manifestation of that single inhabiting divine substance: there is no other; whereas in the Bible, God and man, from the beginning, are distinct. Man is made in the image of God, indeed, and the breath of God has been breathed into his nostrils; yet his being, his self is not that of God, nor is it one with the universe".[81] He stresses that man's separation is an integral theme of the dominant Western thought system: "On the one hand: the power of God who is great, against whom all such merely human categories break as mercy, justice, goodness and love; and, on the other: the titanic builder of the City of Man, who has stolen heavenly fire, courageous and willing to bring upon himself the responsibility of his own decisions. These are the two discordant great themes of what may be termed the orthodox Occidental mythological structure: the poles of experience of an ego set apart from nature, maturing values of its own, which are not those of the given world, yet still projecting on the universe a notion of anthropomorphic fatherhood..."[82]

The blame is not all laid at the door of the Judeo-Christian tradition, however. Campbell suggests that a switch from moon to sun worship, symbolised in Egypt by the replacement of the bull by the lion as principal object of veneration in around 2630BC, was significant. "An age had passed: that of the bull. Another had dawned: that of the lion. The mythology of the lunar bull was henceforth to be overlaid, and not alone in Egypt, by a solar mythology of the lion. The lunar light waxes and wanes. That of the sun is forever bright. Darkness inhabits the moon, where its play is symbolic of that of death in life here on earth, whereas darkness attacks the sun from without and is thrown off daily in defeat by a force that is never dark. The moon is the lord of growth, the waters, the womb, and the mysteries of time; the sun, of the brilliance of the intellect, sheer light, and eternal laws that never change".[83]

He also highlights the replacement of goddess with god as the main deity, reflecting a switch from matriarchy to patriarchy: "And with the progressive devaluation of the mother-goddess in favor of the father, which everywhere accompanied the maturation of the dynastic state and patriarchy but was carried further in Southwest Asia than anywhere else (culminating in the mythology of the Old Testament, where there is no mother-goddess whatsoever), a sense of essential separation from the supreme value symbol became in time the characteristic religious sentiment of the entire Near East. And the rising ziggurats, striving to reach upward in tendance, while at the same time offering to the heavenly powers a ladder by which to come graciously down to the cut-off race of man, were the earliest signals of this spiritual break".[84]

Zerzan sees religious artifice of any kind as a barrier to genuine spiritual connection, identifying the shaman as the precursor of organised religion. He says: "This original specialist became the regulator of group emotions, and as the shaman's potency increased, there was a corresponding decrease in the psychic vitality of the rest of the group".[85] And he writes elsewhere: "Ritual, as shamanic practice, may also be considered as regression from that state in which all shared a consciousness we would now classify as extrasensory. When specialists alone claim access to such perceptual heights as may have once been communal, further backward moves in division of labor are facilitated or enhanced. The way back to bliss through ritual is a virtually universal mythic theme, promising the dissolution of measurable time, among other joys. This theme of ritual points to an absence that it falsely claims to fill, as does symbolic culture in general".[86]

Jung writes: "I am therefore of the opinion that, in general, psychic energy or libido creates the God-image by making use of archetypal patterns, and that man in consequence worships the psychic force active within him as something divine".[87] In this way, the construct of religion comes between humans and their direct access to the greater unity of nature of which they form part.

However, religion is not the only artifice that obscures our view of the universe, as Zerzan for one is at pains to point out. He traces our separation back to the beginnings of agriculture, domestication and symbolic thought. He writes: "It is our fall from a simplicity and fullness of life directly experienced, from the sensuous moment of knowing, which leaves a gap that the symbolic can never bridge. This is what is always being covered over by layers of cultural consolations, civilized detouring that never recovers lost wholeness".[88] He declares: "Symbolic culture inhibits human communication by blocking and otherwise suppressing channels of sensory awareness"[89] and adds: "Culture has led us to betray our own aboriginal spirit and wholeness, into an ever-worsening realm of synthetic, isolating, impoverished estrangement".[90]

Zerzan includes language as part of this alienating symbolic culture: "Verbal communication is part of the movement away from a face-to-face social reality, making feasible physical separateness... Communication outside civilization involved all the senses, a condition linked to the key gatherer-hunter traits of openness and sharing. Literacy ushered us into the society of divided and reduced senses, and we take this sensory deprivation for granted as if it were a natural state, just as we take literacy for granted".[91]

Tolle also sees mental abstraction as separation, arguing: "When you live in a world deadened by mental abstraction, you don't sense the aliveness of the universe anymore. Most people don't inhabit a living reality, but a conceptualized one".[92] And, like Zerzan, he identifies danger in the use of language: "Words and concepts split life into separate segments that have no reality in themselves. We could even say that the notion 'my life' is the original delusion of separateness, the source of ego. If I and life are two, if I am separate from life, then I am separate from all things, all beings, all people. But how could I be separate from life? What 'I' could there be apart from life, apart from Being? It is utterly impossible. So there is no such thing as 'my life' and I don't have a life. I am life. I and life are one".[93] Tolle points the finger at the ego itself: "Ego arises when your sense of Beingness, of 'I Am', which is formless consciousness, gets mixed up with form. This is the meaning of identification. This is forgetfulness of Being, the primary error, the illusion of absolute separateness that turns reality into a nightmare".[94]

At this juncture, we seem to have arrived back at the point where we discussing the non-existence of the individual in the context of a universal entity. It is clear that our mental separation from this whole has been progressive and multi-faceted over many thousands of years. That's not to say, of course, that we haven't often been aware of something amiss and felt a strong urge to connect to something bigger than our individual selves. The problem is, though, that this often just makes things a whole lot worse.

It is undoubtedly true that the individual human being is today more isolated than at any stage of our history. Most of us feel quite separate from our neighbours and fellow citizens, let alone the cosmos. The more atomized the society we live in and the more cut off from the whole we become, the greater the sense of pain and loss that forces us to try and create some kind of identity out of this void. Sometimes this effort is focused solely on ourselves – not on how we feel inside but how we imagine we are perceived by others. We might dress a certain way, act a certain way in order to be "accepted" by those around us. We're only fooling ourselves, for we are not really accepted into anything at all, except the narcissistic condition of viewing the outside world as a mirror in which to gaze at our own reflection.

The ego can be extended beyond our own person to include significant others. Some couples find meaning in a close relationship to the extent that they are psychologically dependent on one another and effectively turn their backs on the rest of the world. Children can be included within the fold, making a kind of collective entity out of the nuclear family, on a temporary basis. Sometimes we specifically seek acceptance from a certain section of our community – others who dress the same way, listen to the same music, drive the same model of car, follow the same football team.

There is nothing wrong with this, in itself. It's important to join in with others in all aspects of our daily lives and the feeling of belonging that this engenders must be beneficial to the mental health of all those involved. The trouble is, though, that on its own this type of connection is fatally flawed. At its heart, it represents an extension of the very sense of isolation and separation that makes it so desperately sought-after. This kind of identity is based on opposition to something else that lies beyond that collective unit. Lacking its own natural sense of self, it defines itself primarily in terms of what it is not. Rather than moving beyond the limitations of the ego, we simply extend it further out into the world around us. Rather than opening up to the vastness of the universe, we close in on ourselves, on our chosen collectivity.

We have already encountered Kropotkin's view of the unnaturalness of the family as primary human unit and how it led to "the individual accumulation of wealth and power, and the hereditary transmission of both".[95] There is something inherently selfish about a family, something that looks inward to a restricted and self-serving outlook rather than outward to the greater picture. This criticism is sometimes extended to tribal communities, whose rejection of outsiders can indeed form a shadow side to the internal solidarity that so appealed to Kropotkin and others. But a tribe provides a big enough space in which to live and develop and at the same time is small enough to have a very human identity – no abstraction is needed to bind it together and, importantly, no external "other" in opposition to which it can define its sense of being.

The same cannot be said for another form of collective identity that has proved very attractive for lost, separated, individuals in search of something to feel a part of – nationalism and, by extension, racialism. The Invisible Committee observe: "The Frenchman, more than anyone else, is the embodiment of the dispossessed, the destitute. His hatred of foreigners is based on his hatred of himself as a foreigner... We have arrived at a point of privation where the only way to feel French is to curse the immigrants and those who are more visibly foreign. In this country, the immigrants assume a curious position of sovereignty: if they weren't here, the French might stop existing".[96] As well as separating humans from each other under the pretence of bringing them together, nationalism and patriotism also play a key role in creating an attitude of submission to the state, presented as a practical incarnation of "the nation". Once people allow themselves to fall for this cheap conjurer's trick and surrender control of their own existence to this phoney deity, they lose the vital force of their collective spirit – their *Geist*, in Landauer's terms.

Writes Landauer: "The state, with its police and all its laws and its contrivances for property rights, exists for the people as a miserable replacement for *Geist* and for organizations with specific purposes; and now the people are supposed to exist for the sake of the state, which pretends to be some sort of ideal structure and a purpose in itself, to be *Geist*... Earlier there were corporate groups, clans, gilds, fraternities, communities, and they all interrelated to form society. Today there is coercion, the letter of the law, the state".[97]

Nation-states thus not only form no part of the connection to the whole which we are attempting to explore, but they also stand in direct opposition to it. But does this mean there is no place for any kind of cultural identity – whether supernational, national or regional? This was certainly an area of contention that much exercised the mind of Landauer, who regarded a *Volk* as very much part of the organic structure of human society. With his concurrent belief in a universal collective identity, he drew a careful line between rejoicing in his own cultural heritage and letting it assume too great a significance. He wrote as part of his contribution to a Zionist compilation: "Strong emphasis on one's own nationality, even when it does not lead to chauvinism, is weakness".[98] This is the key here – the "strong emphasis" placed on a particular collective identity which allows it to overshadow other connections. Landauer once wrote that as a German, a South German and a Jew, he belonged to three "nations" at the same time.[99] The same is true for all of us. The football fan should be able to feel a part of his own club's support without losing track of the fact that he is bonded to rival fans in other aspects of his life – cultural, social or economic.

Likewise, the healthier forms of nationalism are those which incorporate an internationalist outlook – Scottish, Quebecois or Basque nationalism spring to mind as examples, or the anti-imperialist nationalism of the exploited Third

World. There is still the inherent danger that if they achieve their aims they will end up creating a state of their own and thus killing off their animating spirit, but in the stage of liberationary struggle, at least, this kind of urge to self-determination cannot be viewed as harmful.

The important thing to bear in mind is that we are all connected to each other and the universe in a myriad of ways. The various identities we share with others do not neatly radiate out from the individual, via the family, to the community, region, nation and planet, but are much more complex and overlapping. It is only by remaining aware of this at all times that we can avoid the pitfalls of associating too closely with one particular collective identity over all the others or of regarding one of our identities as more valid than someone else's.

It is this sense of a wider belonging, and thus responsibility, which provides us with an ethical dimension to our lives. And ethics, defined in this way, are an important way of assessing whether any particular form of collective identity is a healthy one. Pedler, for instance, argues that the dominant industrial system can itself be seen as a kind of organism, as much as any traditional human society. He explains: "So we now have an emergent robot state, which I have called the cybernarchy. It is as if a new mega-individual has evolved somewhere in the gap between political leaders and people, and it is pursuing a course of self-perpetuation regardless of any other consideration. This mega-individual is a feltwork of flesh and micro-chips, looking after itself at the expense of people".[100]

From our ethical point of view – determining whether a particular collective entity embraces and enhances the health of the whole – this robot state is obviously not a good thing. But sometimes the situation is not so immediately clear-cut. Tolle, for example, comes up with a strange example of what it means to connect with the greater essence of things. He writes: "I have met teachers, artists, nurses, doctors, scientists, social workers, waiters, hairdressers, business owners, and salespeople who perform their work admirably without any self-seeking, fully responding to whatever the moment requires of them. They are one with what they do, one with the Now, one with the people or the task they serve".[101] The implications of this statement are alarming. Does he not think it matters if his scientists are, for instance, testing branded cosmetics on animals or developing toxic chemicals? Is it of no account to him if his business owners are selling cluster bombs to drop on innocent men, women and children who happen to have got in the way of imperial conquest? Is it relevant if his salespeople are selling pointless goods, produced by slave labour, to people who can't really afford them? Is it not important to Tolle who it is that these individuals "serve", whether the "task" that so consumes them is in the interests of the planet or of a destructive global corporation?

From what he writes elsewhere, it clearly is. And yet he has fallen into the trap, on this occasion, of regarding all connection to others as just as positive as connection to the whole. This is the trap that leads others to promote the welfare of their own family to the detriment of the wider community, to espouse nationalism to the detriment of humanity, or, indeed, to pursue the short-term interests of humanity to the detriment of the long-term future of the natural world.

We have already looked at the general idea of being part of a Cosmic Whole, as reflected in various strands of religious, social and scientific thought. We have looked at the idea of immortality as the other side of the coin to the theoretical non-existence of the separate individual. We then went on to view ways in which people have become separated from the awareness of belonging to a bigger organism and the dangers of desperate attempts to plug themselves back in again by identifying with phoney collectivities. These fake organisms, of which nation-states are a prime example, attempt to solve individual alienation by fabricating an identity defined in opposition to another part of the whole, with the result that the holistic overview remains lost and the individual's sense of dislocation is certainly not resolved and is probably even deepened.

It would now be useful to look at how this connection between individuals, apparently such a core part of our existence, is seen by its proponents as functioning. Marshall sets out the theoretical basis: "Living systems, it is now clear, do not form hierarchies but rather networks at different levels. An ecosystem is a network of organisms, in which each organism forms a node, with each node itself a network of organs and so on".[102] But if living creatures, including humans, form these networks, what is it that actually links them together? What connects the nodes? For Landauer it is *Geist*, his invisible spirit or principle. He writes: "A level of great culture is reached when manifold, exclusive and independent communal organizations exist contemporaneously, all impregnated with a uniform *Geist*, which does not reside in the organizations nor arise from them, but which holds sway over them as an independent and self-evident force. In other words, a level of great culture develops when the unifying principle in the diversity of organizational forms and supraindividual structures is not an external bond of force, but a *Geist* inherent in the individuals, directing their attention beyond earthly and material interests".[103]

Jung adopts a similar tone when he refers to "that mysterious and irresistible power which comes from the feeling of being part of the whole".[104] Marais came to the conclusion that something of that kind was operating within the termite communities. He experimented with dividing termitaries in two with steel plates, so the insects could neither see nor contact each other, and found to his amazement that they still continued building matching structures on each side. He remarks that "the functioning of the community or group-psyche of the termitary is just as wonderful and mysterious to a human being, with a very different kind of psyche, as telepathy or other functions of the human mind which border on the supernatural".[105]

Sheldrake cites Marais's work in setting out his theory of morphic fields that provide the invisible connections between apparently separate individual living creatures. He adds: "If the behaviour of social insects is coordinated by a kind of field so far unrecognized by biology and physics, experiments with social insects could tell us something about the properties and nature of such fields, which may well be at work at all levels of social organization, including our own".[106] Writing of the links between beings, he says: "I propose that these bonds are not just metaphorical but real connections. They continue to link individuals together even when they are separated, beyond the range of sensory communication. These connections at a distance could be channels for telepathy".[107]

Sheldrake says his morphic fields, enabling telepathic communication, would explain the closely co-ordinated movements of a school of fish or a flock of birds. He refers to naturalist Edward Selous's studies of the behaviour of birds over a period of 30 years. Like Marais with his termites, Selous became convinced the flocks' collective behaviour could not be explained in terms of normal sensory communication: "I ask how, without some process of thought transference so rapid as to amount practically to simultaneous collective thinking, are these things to be explained?"[108]

Sheldrake proposes that morphic fields could account for animals' well-documented homing instincts and suggests that humans, too, had the same innate ability in our more connected past. He tells of Tupaia, a dispossessed high chief from Tahiti. "Captain James Cook met him in 1769 on his first great voyage of exploration, and invited him to travel on board the Endeavour. During a journey of over 6,000 miles, via the Society Islands, around New Zealand, along the Australian coast and ending in Java, Tupaia was able to point towards

Tahiti at any time, despite the distance involved and the ship's circuitous route between latitudes 48°S and 4°N. By contrast, civilized peoples, and especially modern urban people, have so many artificial aids to navigation, such as signposts, maps and compasses – and now satellite global positioning systems – that a sense of direction is no longer essential to survival".[109]

He also addresses the way information might be passed between successive generations of creatures, focusing on the curious example of the cuckoo. "European cuckoos, raised by birds of other species, do not know their parents," he explains. "In any case, the older cuckoos leave for southern Africa in July or August before the new generation is ready to go. About four weeks later, the young cuckoos find their own way to their ancestral feeding grounds in Africa, unaided and unaccompanied".[110] So how do they know where to go? "One of the features of morphic fields is that they have an inherent memory. This memory is transmitted by a process called morphic resonance, which causes a given organism, such as a migrating bird, to resonate with previous migrating birds of the same kind. Thus when a young cuckoo sets off from England towards Africa, it draws upon a collective memory of its ancestors. This memory, inherent in the morphic field of its migratory path, guides it as it goes, giving it a memory of directions in which to fly, and an instinctive recognition of landmarks, feeding grounds and resting places. This collective memory also enables it to recognize when it has arrived at its destination, the ancestral winter home. Natural selection would strongly favour birds that were sensitive to this ancestral migratory field and migrated in accordance with it. Those that were not in tune with it would probably not survive".[111]

It is important to note that Sheldrake is not ascribing this behaviour to simple genetically-programmed instinct. He argues instead that "animal behaviour can evolve rapidly, as if a collective memory is building up through morphic resonance".[112] Citing some examples, he writes: "The best known involves a series of experiments in which subsequent generations of rats learned how to escape from a water maze. As time went on, rats in laboratories all over the world were able to do this quicker and quicker".[113]

There is no known scientific explanation for rats being able to learn from the experiences of fellow creatures living on the other side of the world. But by proposing telepathy or ESP as a possibility, for humans and animals alike, Sheldrake is in distinguished academic company. Notes Zerzan: "Researchers such as Zohar (1982) consider faculties of telepathy and precognition to have been sacrificed for the sake of evolution into symbolic life. If this sounds far-fetched, the sober positivist Freud (1932) viewed telepathy as quite possibly 'the original archaic means through which individuals understand one another'".[114]

Sheldrake details numerous examples of what, at face value, can only be some kind of telepathic communication between creatures of the same and different species. Whether it is pet animals or spouses "knowing" their loved ones are about to make a move for home, even though many miles away, or the almost universally observed fact that people will, more often than not, look around if you stare at them from behind, he finds that these connections are a definite fact of life, whatever explanation we may care to offer for them. Sheldrake suggests that our thinking and feeling is not in fact carried out by our individual brain, contained within our individual head, but by an extended mind not limited to our physical person. He declares: "Above all, the recognition that our minds extend beyond our brains liberates us. We are no longer imprisoned within the narrow compass of our skulls, our minds separated and isolated from each other. We are no longer alienated from our bodies, alienated from our environment, and alienated from other species. We are interconnected".[115]

Lorimer makes the same case, arguing that our

consciousness does not reside in our brain at all, but in a separate collective psyche, and says "telepathy, clairvoyance and psychometry open up the life experience of other people to the mind of the sensitive, indicating that on one level our minds are not as separate as common sense would suggest".[116]

He also echoes Sheldrake's theory of some kind of collective "field": "Although we are inseparable from the Field, which constitutes our underlying identity as revealed in unitive consciousness, we are nevertheless distinct in form and may have the sensory illusion that we are in fact quite independent".[117] Lorimer describes the case of a woman who had a near-death experience in which she felt that everybody existed in a vast "sea or soup of each other's energy residue and thought waves". He adds: "The only picture within which the above account makes sense is one of an interconnected web of creation, a holographic mesh in which the parts are related to the Whole and through the Whole to each other by empathetic resonance. It must be the sort of Whole in which we and the rest of creation live and move and have our being, a consciousness-field in which we are interdependent strands. It is precisely this oneness and connectedness with the rest of humanity and creation that is the basis of our responsibility: if we were not connected, there could be no possible feedback loop of the kind described above, no tuning in to the memory and consciousness of other forms of life".[118]

The use of the word "responsibility" is interesting here. It necessarily follows that if we are part of a bigger entity, then we should be acting in the interests of that entity as a whole and not merely in those of our limited individual form. This is the same ethical dimension that is missing from identities that are little more than an extension of the ego. Let's now examine how some people manage to tune in to the collective context of their personal responsibility. For it is all very well to theorise that we are all parts of a greater organic whole, but tapping into that elusive feeling, achieving what Indians term *moksa*, or release from delusion, is another matter entirely.

"To achieve the interior act, one must assemble all one's powers, as it were, into one corner of one soul, where, secreted from images and forms, one is able to work," teaches Meister Eckhart. "We must sink into oblivion and ignorance. In this silence, this quiet, the Word is heard. There is no better method of approaching this Word than in silence, in quiet: we hear it and know it aright in unknowing. To one who knows nothing, it is clearly revealed".[119] Says Tolle: "When you contemplate the unfathomable depth of space or listen to the silence in the early hours just before sunrise, something within you resonates with it as if in recognition. You then sense the vast depth of space as your own depth, and you know that precious stillness that has no form to be more deeply who you are than any of the things that make up the content of your life".[120]

"From earth and sea and sun, from night, the stars, from day, the trees, the hills, from my own soul – from these I think," writes Jefferies.[121] He describes how he was brought to a mystical spiritual level on the Downs in the summer: "Sometimes on lying down on the sward I first looked up at the sky, gazing for a long time till I could see deep into the azure and my eyes were full of the colour; then I turned my face to the grass and thyme, placing my hands at each side of my face so as to shut out everything and hide myself. Having drunk deeply of the heaven above and felt the most glorious beauty of the day, and remembering the old, old, sea, which (as it seemed to me) was but just yonder at the edge, I now became lost, and absorbed into the being or existence of the universe. I felt down deep into the earth under, and high above into the sky, and farther still to the sun and stars. Still farther beyond the stars into the hollow of space, and losing thus my separateness of being came to seem like part of the whole".[122] Later he writes: "I was sensitive to all things, to the earth under, and the star-hollow round about; to the least blade of grass, to the largest oak. They seemed like exterior nerves and veins for the conveyance of feeling to me. Sometimes a very ecstasy of exquisite enjoyment of the entire visible universe filled me".[123]

While Jefferies found the answer in nature and Eckhart in silence, countless generations of humans have turned to music as the door to a higher state of consciousness. Writes Campbell: "There were a number of harps found among the suttee-burials of the royal tombs of Ur that bore as ornament the figure of the dead and resurrected moon-bull, Tammuz, with lapis-lazuli beard. For the inaudible 'music of the spheres', which is the hum of the cosmos in being, becomes audible through music; it is the harmony, the meaning, of the social order; and the harmony of the soul itself discovers therein its accord. This idea is basic to Confucian music, to Indian music as well; it was, of course, the Pythagorean belief; and it was a fundamental thought, also, of our own Middle Ages: whence the continuous chanting of the monks, who were diligently practicing in accord with the choir of the angels".[124]

"It is difficult to define this *je ne sais quoi* which suddenly erupts; it is *duende*, it is soul," writes Marshall. "Those who have experienced it often describe it as if it were a creative energy which does not come from them but through them. It is as if some greater force is using you as a channel. You are no longer playing music; music is playing you. You are singing a deep song; you have soul".[125]

In our civilization, we tend to rely on specialists to help us bridge the gulf between mundane individual experience and a greater whole – not just musicians, but also artists, poets and writers. But with that privileged cultural role also comes responsibility. Maurer describes Landauer's thoughts on the matter: "In the ability to combine sense experience with the awareness of self as a manifestation of the universe Landauer recognized the true artistic spirit. It must never be forgotten that the difference between the artist and the masses is one of awareness, not of essence; for the artist, like everyone else, is the product of his *Volk*. Every individual is as much a part of the universal psyche as any other, but most people are not conscious of the relationship. The artist has the power in his creative ability to awaken this consciousness in others".[126]

Writes Landauer himself: "It was individuals, inwardly mighty ones, representatives of the *Volk*, who gave birth to *Geist* in the *Volk*; now it lives in inspired individuals, who consume themselves in their might, who are without *Volk*: isolated thinkers, poets, and artists who without support, as if uprooted, seem to stand on air... All the concentration, all the form that lives within them, powerfully painful, often stronger and larger than their body and soul can bear, the innumerable figures and the color and swarming and thronging of rhythm and harmony; all that – listen you artists! – is stifled *Volk*, is living *Volk*, that has gathered within you, that is buried within you and will arise from within you".[127]

For Landauer, artists were parts of the organic human whole with the ability to channel the life force itself and might resuscitate the moribund, disconnected society in which he found himself living. He declares: "We are poets; and we want to eradicate the science-swindlers, the Marxists, the cold, hollow, spiritless men, so that poetic vision, artistically motivated creating, enthusiasm, and prophecy find the places where from now on they must work, create, build; in life, with human bodies, for communal life, work, and cooperation of groups, communities, peoples..."[128] Landauer also discovers an apparent paradox: "In order not to be an individual, alone in the universe and God-forsaken, I recognize the universe and thereby give up my individuality; but only so as to feel myself as the universe into which I am absorbed".[129]

The French writer Albert Camus explores the same double aspect of the artist's role as an individual. He explains: "To me art is not a solitary delight. It is a means of stirring the greatest number of men by providing them with a privileged image of our common joys and woes. Hence it forces the artist not to isolate himself; it subjects him to the humblest and most universal truth. And the man who, as often happens, chose the path of art because he was aware of his difference soon learns that he can nourish his art, and his difference, solely by admitting his resemblance to all. The artist fashions himself in that ceaseless oscillation from himself to others, midway between the beauty he cannot do without and the community from which he cannot tear himself".[130] And he argues that "at the very moment when the artist chooses to share the fate of all he asserts the individual he is".[131]

We reach an important point here. We have heard that the individual may not even really exist and that the core importance is to feel a connection with the whole. But in trying to find out how this connection can be made, we find that a specific personal sensitivity and mental strength is required and thus, for all the talk of collective organisms and communality, a sense of individuality is crucial. Kropotkin, for one, is in no doubt about this. He writes: "It will probably be remarked that mutual aid, even thought it may represent one of the factors of evolution, covers nevertheless one aspect only of human relations; that by the side of this current, powerful though it may be, there is, and always has been, the other current – the self-assertion of the individual, not only in its efforts to maintain personal or caste superiority, economical, political and spiritual, but also in its much more important although less evident function of breaking through the bonds, always prone to become crystallized, which the tribe, the village community, the city, and the State impose upon the individual. In other words, there is the self-assertion of the individual taken as a progressive element".[132]

Camus likewise argues that individual rebellion, on a political level, is in fact operating to the benefit of the whole: "Only he who is uncompromising as to his rights maintains the sense of duty. The great citizens of a country are not those who bend their knee before authority but rather those who, against authority if need be, are adamant as to the honour and freedom of that country".[133] Seen in more general terms, the freedom of an individual appears as an aspect of the flexibility and diversity that maintains the balance of the overall whole. Pedler, for instance, argues that "stability within Gaia, or within one of her parts such as an ecosystem, is partly maintained by species diversity".[134] Lovelock also describes the way that diversity results in a stronger and more stable ecosystem and comments that it "seems likely that the biosphere diversified rapidly as it evolved".[135]

In other words, the existence of individual species and individual members of those species is part of a deliberate strategy of diversification by the parent organism, whether we see that as Gaia or the entire universe. We do not exist as individuals randomly, because of some kind of break-down or mistake on behalf of the greater entity to which we owe our existence, but because this entity functions best by splitting itself into diverse parts.

Marais, in his observation of baboons, discerns a crucial break from the behaviour of other mammals – let alone birds, fish or insects – in that individuals are able to adapt to different environments rather than follow inherited patterns of behaviour. He writes of this important psychological change: "The first and most important step is to wipe out the inherited or race memory. Unless this happens there can be no change in environment. Not only must the race memory be destroyed, but even the possibility of its being inherited must disappear from the psyche – or the change will be useless. Instead of race memory a psyche must be developed which enables every individual to acquire his own causal memory of his environment. It is this change in the baboons which has given them an advantage which every one who is familiar with them will concede".[136]

The same obviously applies to the human race and means that with their flexibility and capacity for autonomous action, human individuals have a special responsibility to play in shaping the evolution and direction of the whole. Asks Lovelock: "If we are a part of Gaia it becomes interesting to ask: 'To what extent is our collective intelligence also a part of Gaia? Do we as a species constitute a Gaian nervous system and a brain which can consciously anticipate environmental changes?'"[137] But there is a downside to this new role, as Marais points out. He refers to "serious psychological disorders" caused by the inhibition and sudden release of the old animal psyche. And he warns: "The baboon and man paid an exorbitant price for their new type of psyche – a price which is bound surely but slowly to bring about their natural extermination".[138]

Lovelock, like many others, is all too aware of the menace presented by humanity's rampant individualism and mental disconnection from the whole. However, he disappointingly fails to see through the obvious implications of his notion that humanity could represent some kind of planetary nervous system. Recognizing that we form part of Gaia and thus of nature, he regards everything that happens on Earth as intrinsically natural, including the likes of nuclear power and pollution and repeatedly attacks environmental objections to them. He writes, for instance: "To grass, beetles, and even farmers, the cow's dung is not pollution but a valued gift. In a sensible world, industrial waste would not be banned but put to good use. The negative, unconstructive response of prohibition by law seems as idiotic as legislating against the emission of dung from cows".[139]

Again and again, Lovelock takes the view that Gaia will sort out any problems, even man-made ones, and we don't need to lift a finger to do anything about it. One example he cites is the way in which the planet once reacted to the arrival of oxygen in the atmosphere, which was, he says, essentially "poisonous" to the existing biosphere. He concludes: "Ingenuity triumphed and the danger was overcome, not in the human way by restoring the old order, but in the flexible Gaian way by adapting to change and converting a murderous intruder into a powerful friend".[140] This argument, first published in 1979, still appears in the 2000 edition of his famous book, albeit with a note admitting that it had turned out to be a little inaccurate: "We now think that oxygen did not appear suddenly but grew from mere traces at the start of life to its present day abundance. This gave time for adaptation".[141] He seems bizarrely oblivious to the fact that this revelation completely undermines his whole argument!

Regardless of that eccentricity, the main point that Lovelock so obviously misses is that if man-made problems, such as pollution, are completely natural and all part of Gaia's mysterious ways, then so are man-made solutions. This does not just mean the anti-pollution legislation that, for whatever reason, he so vehemently opposes, but any other form of human opposition to environmental destruction, ranging from voting for environmentally-conscious politicians through to carrying out direct action sabotage on the offending industries. It's all part of human life and thus all part of the workings of Gaia.

Indeed if the health of the planet is really threatened by the ill effects of man-made activity, as we know it is, then what other Gaian element but humanity is best placed to bring an end to the damage and begin a global healing process? And the means by which humanity will achieve this can only be through its individuals, evolved to possess the will and flexibility to try and shape the world for better as well as for worse.

The whole point of nature giving us personal freedom and individuality is to give us the choice as to whether we want to go along with the status quo, accept the direction our species or planetary superorganism is taking, or whether we want to try and change it. We, as human beings, can act as the antennae which sense danger, the control mechanisms which prevent disaster for the whole. The fact that there are some human beings who are working in the opposite direction makes no difference to the role we have to play – in fact, it makes it even more important that we do so, rather than just sit back and wait for some other part of our planet to make things right, as Lovelock so insidiously recommends.

When a healthy human body comes under attack from antigens – harmful substances such as bacteria, fungi, parasites, viruses or chemicals – it doesn't just lie back and allow itself to be killed off. Its immune system, if it has not been compromised by ill health, produces antibodies specifically designed to fight that particular threat. Some human beings and their activities are acting as antigens, threatening the health of our species and our planetary superorganism. Other humans, in whom a sense of individual freedom is combined with a responsibility for the well-being of the whole, must therefore take on the role of antibodies.

"In much the same way as the malignant cells of cancer invade and destroy the normal tissue of the body, so do the affairs and processes of the toymaker technocrats invade and destroy the balanced and stable earth organism,"[142] writes Pedler, in a passage that indicates why his Gaian work is less publicised than Lovelock's. And he warns of the dire consequences of us not taking seriously our responsibility for the well-being of the whole: "I have used the myth of the goddess Gaia to express the idea that we are an integral part of a single, intelligent life-form which acts like an individual. I have tried to show how it is that we can never separate ourselves from this life-form, despite our delusions of dominance and control, because should we succeed in doing so, we would be committing an irreversible act of mass suicide: as if an arm tried to exist separately from the body".[143]

But concern for the environment is not the only sphere of action which must, inevitably and logically, form part of a socio-political immune system for Gaia. We have already seen how co-operation is a fundamental principle of life itself and therefore of healthy human societies. In order for humanity to fulfil its potential, and become a positive asset to the planet rather than an unpleasant disease, our societies must be able to function in the way they are meant to function. The destruction of organic human communities is itself part of the illness afflicting the whole of Gaia and cannot be separated from it. The Earth's immune system is not working because the natural flows of energy in our societies have been blocked by impediments.

If our society is not based on mutual aid – on generally helping each other rather than blindly following what we wrongly perceive to be in our own personal interest – then it is not an authentic human society and will not behave in the way that an authentic society has evolved to behave. We see all too clearly today that the promotion of greed (under the guise of "enterprise" or "wealth creation") is the driving force behind the environmental destruction being wrought. We live in a society that promotes and rewards selfish behaviour and which discourages solidarity on even the lowest level.

All power must be seen to ultimately derive from the state, the most pernicious of those fake collectivities we discussed earlier. Resources are forcibly extracted from populations in the form of taxation and then partly restored to them in the form of "funding" that must always be seen to be some kind of gift from authority. No kind of independence from this central structure can be allowed, no corner of humanity can be exempt from its demands and its rules. This is nothing short of a calamity. In the same way as an acorn will not grow into an oak tree if it is confined indoors in a flower pot, so can the human collective organism never become what it is meant to be if it is not able to draw upon the full strength of its inborn resources. All layers of authority, particularly states and governments, block the emergence of human collective genius, block our vital flexibility, block the ways in which our species could emerge as a healing force despite the damage we have inflicted.

There is more than one meaning to democracy. On one hand it can be the narrow, limited and phoney exercise of seeming to allow the population control of its own affairs by persuading it to ritually surrender its sovereignty to "representatives" selected from among the ruling elite. On the other hand it can be the manner in which a collective sense of purpose, a collective response, is drawn from the depths of a community and allowed to steer that community in the direction which the whole organism feels is the right one. The first type of democracy, an intrinsic part of the state's dictatorship, is one of the ways in which the second type of democracy is put out of action.

Not only does the very structure of our society destroy the collective identity, the morphic field, the *Geist* that makes humans communities amount to so much more than the sum of the individuals they contain, but it also sets out to deliberately prevent this sorry state of affairs from ever changing. Contemporary human society is so diseased that it actively disables its own immune system. The very antibodies which could save the ailing superorganism are categorised as the enemy within, as criminal threats to the state in its devious guise as a genuine collective whole.

"What the mind likes to be is free and prohibition of this freedom is called obstruction to the nature,"[144] declares a third century AD Taoist text and the freedom of the human species to be its natural self is obstructed by entities which physically prevent democracy, the conscience of the whole. So as well as fighting against physical injury to the living flesh of our planet, and seeking to dismantle the unnatural structure of a society which prevents us from accessing our own collective powers of self-healing, we find ourselves necessarily engaged in a war of resistance against the forces of reaction and repression whose narrow interests lie in maintaining our deadly descent into disaster.

Because the impulse to solidarity and freedom comes naturally to human beings, and emerges powerfully in generation after generation, the forces of repression must constantly deploy their powers to prevent it challenging their tyranny. From the brutal use of military might to put down popular uprisings over the centuries, through the bans on workers "combining" in trade unions in the 19th century, to the criminalisation of dissent so prevalent today, a permanent struggle is taking place. If everything was functioning as it should, this would not be necessary. The sensitive antennae of the human race would transmit subtle messages through our communities which would modify our behaviour, genuine democracy would prevail and conflict would not be necessary. But as things are, it is simply not possible for even a majority of a population to alter the course steered, in their own interests, by the few who have seized unaccountable power and are prepared to use any means to hold onto it.

This is not a pleasant reality to have to confront and, as Zerzan points, many well-meaning people are in complete denial over how dire the situation has become, both for democracy and for the planet. He says: "This denial is not going to be changed by little reforms, and the planet is not going to be saved by recycling. To think it will is just silly. Or no, it's not silly, it's criminal. We have to face what's going on. Once we've faced reality then we can together figure out how to change it, how to completely transform it".[145] Fellow environmentalist Derrick Jensen writes: "Begging government and industry to stop destroying the planet and to stop killing people the world over is never going to work. It can't".[146]

But how then do we resist these malevolent forces? What does resistance involve? How far can we take this? The answer has to be that we must take it as far as we have to, in order to overcome the obstructions placed in our way. Because the flow of information is generally controlled by states and their business partners, dissidents have created their own media, notably on the internet. Because the conventional democratic process is so easily exhausted without any noticeable effect on the machineries of destruction, radicals take to the streets to get their message across. Because dissent is criminalised by the state and protesters are intimidated with everything from surveillance to outright physical violence, others find covert direct action a useful avenue. Because the state employs thousands of people to monitor, infiltrate and disrupt its opponents, many of them have taken to operating in autonomous "affinity groups" rather than larger visible organisations.

Every time the levels of repression move up a notch, so must the levels of resistance, otherwise the antibodies have failed in their job. There is no obvious end to this process. If some means of dissent are blocked, other forms acquire immediate moral legitimacy. Is there anybody who would argue that the armed French resistance against the Nazi occupation was not a proportionate and necessary response? Is there any cause more compelling than the survival of the planet and the liberty of the human immune system to perform its natural function? Explains Pedler: "If the capacity for responsibility is expropriated by a non-representative state, then it follows that violent revolution must take place, since there is no other way of changing the situation".[147]

"If a man reckons the unconscious as part of his personality, then one must admit that he is in fact raging against himself," writes Jung. "But, in so far as the symbolism thrown up by his suffering is archetypal and collective, it can be taken as a sign that he is no longer suffering from himself, but rather from the spirit of the age. He is suffering from an objective, impersonal cause, from his collective unconscious which he has in common with all men".[148] Says Tolstoy: "The anguish of suffering is only that pain which men experience on their attempt to break that chain of love to their ancestors, to their descendants, to their contemporaries, which unites the life of a man with the life of the world".[149]

Are we coming close now to understanding why so many of our lives are mired in despair and how we can conquer that darkness and live as we know we should be living? Lorimer argues: "A worldview which fragments reality necessarily disconnects people from their context and leads directly to a lack of meaning. Conversely, a world-view which connects life, matter and consciousness to an underlying process reinstates the sense of meaning and overcomes fragmentation".[150]

Camus, writing in the resistance newspaper *Combat* on August 25 1944, revels in the joy that has been instilled by the long and arduous struggle against oppression in which he and his comrades have been engaged: "United in the same suffering for four years, we still are united in the same intoxification; we have won our solidarity. And we are suddenly astonished to see during this dazzling night that for four years we have never been alone. We have lived the years of fraternity".[151]

Did the collective intoxification of the resistance fighters come about *despite* the fact that individuals among them faced death and indeed were killed? Or did it come about *because* of this? Tolstoy writes: " Death, to the man who should live only for others, could not seem to be a cessation of happiness and life, because the happiness and the life of other beings is not only not interrupted with the life of a man who saves them, but is frequently augmented and heightened by the sacrifice of his life".[152] "A free man thinks of nothing less than of death," declares Spinoza.[153]

Once we no longer fear our own mortality, secure in the knowledge that our true life lies on a deeper plane than that of our temporary individual form, then our strength knows no bounds. Lao Tzu says in the *Tao Te Ching*: "I have heard it said that one who excels in safeguarding his own life does not meet with rhinoceros or tiger when travelling on land nor is he touched by weapons when charging into an army. There is nowhere for the rhinoceros to pitch its horn; there is nowhere for the tiger to place its claws; there is nowhere for the weapon to lodge its blade. Why is this so? Because for him there is no realm of death".[154]

Any of us can reach this state of mind, as it is our natural condition before we were spiritually cut off from the Whole, from the collective unconscious, from Gaia, from the soul of the superorganism. Kropotkin sees what we term "heroism" as being something basic to human psychology, although it is not always realised: "Unless men are maddened in the battlefield, they 'cannot stand it' to hear appeals for help, and not to respond to them. The hero goes; and what the hero does, all feel that they ought to have done as well. The sophisms of the brain cannot resist the mutual-aid feeling, because this feeling has been nurtured by thousands of years of human social life and hundreds of thousands of years of pre-human life in societies".[155]

All we have to do to access our true human nature, our destined role as antibodies protecting the greater life-form, is to remove the mental blocks that stand in our way – all the trappings of ego, all the attachments to fake identities that blind and mislead us. "Anyone who would be what he ought to be must stop being what he is," writes Meister Eckhart.[156] "A man does not live for happiness, but for the task he chooses. For the sake of that task everything, really everything, must be borne," advises Landauer in a stirring letter to a fellow anarchist.[157] He asks, elsewhere: "What is so important about life? We soon die, we all die, we do not live at all. Nothing lives except what we make of ourselves, what we undertake with ourselves; achievements live; not the creature, only the creator. Nothing lives but the deed of honest hands and the workings of pure, genuine, *Geist*".[158]

And, of course, just as the collective spirit surfaces in the will and the actions of an individual part of the whole, so the individuals who allow their true nature to work within them will feed back energy into the collective and help amplify it still further. The Invisible Committee argues: "Revolutionary movements do not spread by contamination but by resonance. Something that is constituted here resonates within the shock wave emitted by something constituted over there. A body that resonates does so according to its own mode. An insurrection is not like a plague or a forest fire – a linear process which spreads from place to place after an initial spark. It rather takes the shape of a music, whose focal points, though dispersed in time and space, succeed in imposing the rhythm of their own vibrations, always taking on more density. To the point that any return to normal is no longer desirable or even imaginable".[159]

Landauer terms this resonance or music *Wahn* – a kind of human aspiration, an inspiration to move forward. He explains: "*Wahn* is not only every goal, every ideal, every belief in a sense of purpose of life and the world: *Wahn* is every banner followed by mankind; every drumbeat leading mankind into danger; every alliance that unites mankind and creates from a sum of individuals a new structure, an organism. *Wahn* is the greatest thing mankind has; there is always something of love in it: love is *Geist* and *Geist* is love: and love and *Geist* are *Wahn*".[160]

It is this willingness to follow the drumbeat into danger, to cast aside our individual fears and resonate with the whole, that is so crucial both for our own sense of authenticity and for the common good. Too often we hide from the responsibility this entails, from the confrontation and personal risk involved – sometimes, as Zerzan set outs, under the excuse of being "nice". This, he says, is the perfect enemy of tactical or analytical thinking: "Be agreeable; don't let having radical ideas make waves in your personal behavior. Accept the pre-packaged methods and limits of the daily strangulation. Ingrained deference, the conditioned response to 'play by the rules' – authority's rules – this is the real Fifth Column, the one within us".[161]

This hiding, this backing out of our responsibilities, is highly dangerous to our psychological development, as Jung stresses. "Flight from life does not exempt us from the law of age and death," he warns. "The neurotic who tries to wiggle out of the necessity of living wins nothing and only burdens himself with a constant foretaste of aging and dying, which must appear especially cruel on account of the total emptiness and meaninglessness of his life. If it is not possible for the libido to strive forwards, to lead a life that willingly accepts all dangers and ultimate decay, then it strikes back along the other road and sinks into its own depths..."[162]

We are used to seeing depicted in fictional form a willingness to take risks, even to sacrifice oneself for the protection of whole. In the film *Avatar* mentioned earlier, for instance, the threatened planet is saved by the determination of every living creature to hurl itself at the enemy forces, regardless of the individual danger. But when it comes to real life – our own little personal lives with jobs, families, friends and comfortable routines – we seem to need reminding that we have a serious duty to perform.

This duty is not an optional extra but our very *raison d'être* – we are the antibodies that have to defend the health of our superorganism. If we do not act as we know, deep down, we should, then our whole existence becomes nothing but an empty sham, a failure on the most fundamental biological level. As Zerzan says, in a conversation with Jensen: "We didn't make this culture. We didn't turn the world into the battleground and cemetery it has become. We didn't turn human relations into the parody they have become. But now it is our responsibility to overcome what our culture has created. Maybe you could say that now we must be what we must be to overcome it".[163]

WE ANARCHANGELS OF CREATIVE DESTRUCTION

"A giant bird was struggling out of the egg: the egg was the
world and the world must first be rent asunder"

Hermann Hesse[1]

"Anarchy is life; the life that awaits us after we have freed
ourselves from the yoke"

Gustav Landauer[2]

Do not be afraid for we are ANARCHANGELS and we have
risen up from amongst you to set you free and save our world.

We have known for so long that this realm into which we
were forced to become manifest, this civilisation in which we
are all suffocating, is corrupt with rank and wretched decay.

We know this from the dead eyes of the human robots
thronging the passageways of the commuter rail networks, the
factories and the schools.

We know this from the tears of tiny babies propped up in
front of television screens and told to learn how to fit in.[3]

We know this from the despairing cries of the fish, the
birds, and the animals that are choking on the force-fed toxic

excretions of the diabolic god Progress.[4]

We know this from the hellish roar of a billion bulldozers, the tormented wailing of a million passenger jets carrying triumphantly aloft a restless humanity desperately trying to escape the gaping insanity of its soul.[5]

We know this from the computer-readable price tags laser-burnt onto every blade of grass, every butterfly wing, every feeble sapling by the eager adepts of the Cult of Quantity.

We know this from the dripping limbs torn from small children, the blood and the grief and the screams of eternal suffering which are distilled and diverted to fill the bank accounts of the yellow-eyed death-mongers.

We know this from the happy couple Gluttony and Poverty, who march hand in hand round and round the globe to keep up with the daily opening of the international stock exchanges. So sweet together and each so indispensable to the other!

We know this from the fear in the hearts of the powerful, the ignorance in the minds of the dispossessed, the anger in the blood of all those who have seen through it all and yet still can change nothing.

We know this from the prisons, the courts, the surveillance cameras, the baton-wielding slave-thugs always ready to pounce on and destroy any faint stirring of that tender precious freedom called revolt.

We know this from our own despair, our own incomprehension, our own rage, our own failures, our own sorrow, our own deadly yearning to break out of this lonely nightmare for once and for all. We know this because we know. And we know that it must all be destroyed.

"Wait!" you cry. "Most likely you are not angels at all, but merely devils taking on the semblance! Destruction is a black force and not to be wielded lightly by those with a claim to higher motivations!"

We will not hear of this shallow argument. It should be clear from what we just said that our destructive desire flows from the most positive of sources.

Behind our whole critique of this benighted civilisation is a deep sense of value. This may even once have escaped us ourselves, so caught up were we in the emotion and pain of our spiritual dislocation.

But when we look again at that which hurts us most, we see that underlying it all is the absence of the values that we cherish. We worship life, truth, beauty, nature, the freedom of all creatures to live to their potential, a striving towards perfection and an understanding of the cosmic whole.

This civilisation is built on nothing but cancerous growth, on its own self-fulfilling prophecy of endless exploitation, destruction, production, standardisation, isolation, separation, specialisation, centralisation.[6]

It has no ethos, no principle behind it save a barely human grunt for "more, more, more!"[7] Nothing can stand in the way of its addiction as it gorges itself on its own body and spews acid abuse in the face of those who say this cannot go on.

But of course it can never reveal itself to be the beast it is. Instead it turns the picture upside down and presents itself as the protector of values – and ourselves, we Anarchangels, as the threat to all that is good and proper.

These shallow pseudo-values are so lacking in substance that you would perhaps have imagined that nobody could be idiot enough to take them as real. But, sadly, it seems that the malaise of our times includes the descent into witless gullibility of a fair proportion of our fellow citizens.[8]

Thus it was that the mass murderer Hitler persuaded the German people that he was the saviour of their noble culture, by cunning use of pomp and propaganda. Thus it is that the black magicians of contemporary times can have (almost!) an entire people believe that their cultural inheritance, liberties, identity, dignity and future can be represented by a motley collection of historical individuals, events and developments.

Sometimes these are presented proudly in the plastic

packaging of globalised consumerism and on other occasions, when it suits, they are all wrapped up in a musty old piece of multi-coloured cloth. Conveniently in the secure ownership of those who possess wealth and thus power (it works just as well in reverse!), this is presented in itself as a "value" although clearly it is nothing of the sort.[9]

The totem, with nothing in reality behind it other than the need for control over the population, can then be wielded as and when necessary to the desired effect. With one wave of the magic rag, their eyes are drawn away from the conjuror's accomplices busy picking their pockets, stealing the food from their tables, corrupting their children.

And so it is with all these "traditions" and "values" paraded before us by those who merely want to hold on to what they already have. They are empty, without moral content.[10]

Don't ask the meaning of a religion, just obey its rules and keep your mouth and mind closed! Keep telling yourself that the Emperor has a fine set of new clothes otherwise you may find his Anti-Terrorist Squad kicking in your front door!

The "traditions" and "culture" that (just about) hold this civilisation together have the depth of a cinematic stage set, the authenticity of a theme park ride. The judge's wig, the businessman's suit, the monarch's crown are all just flimsy substitutes for real content, real tradition, real value.

Given that this is so, it may seem possible that our own authentic values could be nurtured in such a way as to show up their hollow version for the fraud it is. Why the need for destruction when the new society we crave could be built within the shell of the old and, given its inherent superiority, eventually replace it?[11]

This is a fine idea, and an appealing one, but unfortunately takes no cognisance of the depressing reality at which we have arrived. The system of power understands all too well the threat of an alternative source of value or tradition, the potential of parallel social or cultural structures arising beyond its control. It had to understand this, and defeat it, in order to have achieved its monopoly in the first place.

This is why heretics have been put to death, witches burned, land enclosed, restrictions imposed, education controlled, taxes enforced, borders patrolled, media regulated, dissidents imprisoned, organisations infiltrated, initiatives disrupted, authors discredited, travellers moved on, squats evicted, protests banned, email intercepted, web servers seized, public opinion assiduously manipulated.

The hunger of Progress[12] demands spiralling sacrifices of our planet's living flesh and its servants need ever more power to carry out its orders. If they do not crack the whip and impose its will then they have failed in their appointed task.

Be sure that this system will do just what it has to do in its lust for power. It will stop short of nothing. It is not going to stand idly by and watch us build its replacement under its very nose. It is not going to be won over by the niceness of our actions or the kindness of our tone into letting us get on with a project that it knows could undermine its existence.

The malignant growth we term civilisation is not going to allow healthy cells of life to get in the way of its fatal expansion. It does not intimidate opponents because they are criminals, though that is inevitably its public justification. It does so because they threaten its monopoly and it cares little whether they do so by way of insurrection or agricultural commune. The Diggers of George's Hill had no molotov cocktails concealed beneath their 17th century tunics and still they were crushed under the boot of power.

This does not mean we should not embrace creativity and show by our example that there are better ways to live. But we will always need to be ready to fight to defend our vision. Indeed, we have always needed to be ready to do that.

We have fought over and over again, throughout history. We have to admit we have generally been defeated – otherwise we would not find ourselves where we are today.

But the struggle itself has been a victory of sorts, a flame kept burning and an inspiration for those to come. It is these battles, however tragic their conclusion at the hands of the dark forces, that have given birth to each new generation of Anarchangels. And the overwhelming truth that we draw from these bitter past experiences, in particular from their failure, is that we will never achieve what we want until we have destroyed the system in its entirety.[13]

You don't need us to tell you this. Deep down you knew already, but were unwilling to face up to the enormity of the implications. If your house was structurally unsound, right down to the foundations, would you try putting a new roof on it and seeing if that helped?

If the cancer of this civilisation is not cleansed from our collective body it will return to colonise any new growth we have managed to inspire. It will draw strength from the fresh energy, absorb the juices and rise up again to reimpose its vicious stranglehold.

We Anarchangels know it will not be easy to kill this system, this civilisation. If it was easy it would have been accomplished long ago. But we know that it has to be done and we know that it is our task to try to do it.

We cannot separate in our minds the noble values that inspire us from the means with which we can enable them to prevail against the heavy decay that oppresses us all. We cannot separate them because they are, in fact, the same thing – two aspects of one incandescent guiding star.

If we create an authentic alternative we are, as the powerful know full well, attempting to destroy the current system. And if we attempt to destroy the current system we are, as we Anarchangels know full well, trying to allow the authentic alternative to come into being.

Creation is destruction. Destruction is creation. This is our faith and this is what drives us on towards our destinies.

We listen with interest to those who tell us that this is all meant to be and we are living towards the end of a great cycle of history. The ancient Upanishads tell of a gradual descent from the Golden Age (*Satya Yuga*) to the Dark Age, known as *Kali Yuga*.[14] The age foretold in these writings sounds very much like our own and here we can see its lack of values stripped down and made yet plainer.

Multiplication lies at the heart of it all – move still further from the light of simplicity and everything just falls apart. Religions focus more and more on the detail and the dogma rather than on the eternal truth that inspired them. Science splinters and specialises, focusing on smaller and smaller detail and becoming more interested in the material application of its findings than in how they contribute to our understanding of the universe.

Mass society lends the appearance of unity but in fact its bringing-together is a tearing-apart, as individuals become isolated, addicted to their own egos and have no sense of any selfless role in the working of it all. The writings say that *Kali Yuga* is accelerating ever faster towards its doom, like a stone rolling down a mountainside[15] and that it will end in destruction,[16] followed by the dawning of a new *Satya Yuga*.

We welcome this prediction. But we are also wary of falling for the notion that this is all inevitable and all we must do is sit and wait for epochal fate to run its course.[17] For we know that we have work to do. The water wheel of history will not turn by itself and we are the droplets who must converge to power the change.

We have no real choice in the matter, for this is simply what we have to be – in the same way as an antibody in our blood must set out to combat disease and infection.[18] But that doesn't mean it comes easily, lazily, without effort – and there are some who will drop back, useless and unfulfilled, like a spermatozoon unfit to fertilise an egg.

A fallen anarchangel will plunge, wither and be sucked back into a dark vortex of their own unopened potential, now turned inwards to bitterness and a stunted self. But we others – we angel-droplets, we swim-sprinting spermatozoa, we creative destroyers of the *Kali Yuga* – will play out our role with determination and pride.

How many Anarchangels does it take to bring down a civilisation? More than we are now, that is for sure. But we will swell in size and strength as others flow into our stream and turn it into a mighty river.

Don't forget that it rains all the time. Life-moisture expended and drawn up into the air is formed again and joins us here on Earth. Regeneration means new generations and these are born to play their part in the ending of an age.

The death-power is strong and could not be defeated by the energy of risings past. But each time we come back stronger and in greater numbers. Each time we know less fear and we understand more fully just how far we have to go. This will happen again and again until we have won. *Sin miedo.*[19] Nothing can stop us.

Anarchangels don't just fight to win, we fight to show the way, to sound the trumpet of revolt.[20] Our rage inspires an electric force that draws in others to our rebellion – even babies in the womb are infused with its necessity and grow up to discover why it is they are here and what it is they now must do.

Through this resonance we can transmit from our halo-antennae not just the riotous fury of our cause but the joyful values we uphold. These values we hold dear contain the knowledge that the corrupted present must be rent asunder.

Birth and death. Death and birth. Neither comes first, neither is more important than the other. They are one and that knowledge is what binds us to our duty. And what a duty it is, what a heavy load for any weak mortal to bear.[21]

We must make ourselves strong, fellow Anarchangels, through some alchemy of the soul! First we must descend into the depths of our inner selves to see all that is there and then rise up high and let the dross all drop away.[22] Purified, we float above – but here we cannot rest. Down again, down into the world of men and women so we can be just what we're meant to be.[23]

Now we must speak of our values and how it is that we would hold on to them throughout the great falling of the Darkest Age. Deep down, we know, these values are as much a part of us as we of them and must forever lie inside our souls, all ready to unfold.

All would not be lost, therefore, if every memory of culture were wiped out and we began again, in naked innocence. Eventually, it would all come back to us in our dreams. But we need not waste the precious heritage we own and our aim is to carry it with us through the coming storm.

Just as a civilisation at its peak carries the seed of its own destruction, so a civilisation at its lowest point contains the seed of a future rebirth. We Anarchangels must be custodians of this seed so that we can plant the tree of wisdom in the coming Golden Age.

In one hand we carry the black flag of revolt, in the other the ancient book of wisdom that will serve our children well.[24] Like Ariadne's thread, this knowledge can lead them and us away out of the dark and perplexing labyrinth of earthly existence and into the light of understanding.

These sacred values can't be found on the surface of this dying age. The books that teach them won't be stacked up in Tesco, turned into a three-part mini-series on Channel 4 or liked by millions on Facebook. Our values won't be taught on the National Curriculum or trumpeted by state religions or wrapped up in plastic in the glossy supplement of your bulging Sunday paper.[25]

How could they be? These are the values that our civilisation has to suppress in order to maintain its hegemony![26]

These are the values we began by defending, before the

fury of the struggle itself left us drifting without sight of how it all began.

But although these values are not spelled out in neon lights or declaimed by the high priests of football at half-time in the Champions League Final, they do still exist and can be found. Look – there they are in those old esoteric texts! And there they are in pagan folklore, in gnostic scriptures[27], in indigenous wisdom![28]

There they are on the lips of a wise woman, there they are between the lines of the world's religions, there they are in that inauspicious tome in a secondhand bookshop that somehow, for reasons you can never explain, you find yourself reaching for and taking home to read! And there they are disguised in the clothing of myth![29]

These are our human values, these are our natural values, these are the values by which we are intended to live. If that were not so, they would by now have disappeared down the plughole of the millennia and drained away into a forgotten past.

And when this system is destroyed, when we have played our appointed part in the ending of this *Kali Yuga*, when anarchy has prevailed, when the blockage in the fountainhead has been removed and the spring of life is flowing as it should,[30] then those values will surface again, triumphant and supreme.

The Golden Age will have returned and we Anarchangels will rejoice!

THE TASK

Once when I was living it would all just make me weep – the suffering, the loss, the corruption of the light.

Now I watch as it unfolds and know that this must be – the breaking down of everything we thought we knew was true.

For me it is too late to play a part in what I see and so instead I call upon you, my friend, to take my place.

I know you have no choice for I watch you night and day. I see you wish great yearning strides towards a place where love and warmth will let you share your mortal days with joy.

I see you close your eyes in summer and dream yourself content and real. I see from time to time how the spirit of belonging takes over the moment and blows it to a swirling height of revelation.

But I also see that even then – nay above all then – the shadow makes its presence known and points to this brief bliss as merely what you could have known if all had not been cooped up and curtailed.

I see you blindly try to blind yourself to what you know you see. You have no choice. You cannot live like this, die like this.

You just wanted the truth – could you now be content to while away your dwindling days in a cage made of your own lies, built to protect your shallow ego from the wild risk of exposure to your self?

Will you surround yourself with those you love, all clinging together on the edge of the cliff like frightened baby rabbits? Will you seek confirmation in each other's smiling, selfish eyes that your existence is real and death will never happen?

An ego shared is still a sin and suffocates the soul. So shout it now and shout it loud and tell them all to go away!

You'll have to scream to make it known this is no jest, no passing whim, no sulk or strop of stupid angst. Find true friends – with hatred in their eyes! Seek out those who reject you and let their venom burn away the putrid fat of vanity that shelters you from what you have to know.

What will you be, who will you have been if your flesh expires before you have done what you had always promised yourself you would do, ever since you caught a bedazzling glimpse of the blackness when you were still but a boy?

You staggered away from it then, clutching your head in confusion. Nothing could be the same again and others saw the haunting of your eyes and wondered where that carefree child had fled.

Again and again, I have seen you circle back in on what you know is there and reach out to shock yourself once more with its crackling charge.

Each time I imagine that finally you have seen that you must become what you are and be what you have to be. But, alas, you allow yourself to be distracted by minor tasks and themes and thus your feeble peace of mind remains intact.

Make yourself busy, my friend, so that you simply have no time for what you fear to face! Ha! On and on it goes, this fickle flight from responsibility while all the time you paint yourself a picture in which you are so strong, so brave, so set on going to the very heart of that which lays us low. And all the while, the years slip by and nothing comes to pass.

I've tried to help. I've tried to steer you on to the road you have to take. I gave you signs you may have read but never deigned to follow.

I pushed you hard, I made you crack, I took away your props of home and love and pride. Just then I thought I'd done enough – you seemed to touch the very core and take at last a step towards and not around.

But, again, you wandered off and filled your mind with simple stuff not fit for one whose will would rise so large and true. What will it take, when will you stop this shameful crime against yourself? I know your dreams, those planned and not, and see you often perched atop some lofty tower from which you think to plunge and thus escape the calling of your fate.

But what a joke to climb so high to fall back down to where you were!

The deadly difference, of course, is now your bones are crushed, your flesh dispersed and all you could have been can be no more.

Spare me your self-pity that is nothing but a way to hide the cowardly and loathsome blood you never could admit flowed through your veins! Spare me the self-deception of a self-destruction born of self-indulgence!

It's not the wish to plunge that I deplore, but that your plunge should end so fast and reach not far enough for me. Imagine that you fell indeed, but that the ground had not the strength to break your fall and instead you crashed right through into a world hid out of view.

Beneath the surface of our gold-paved streets you'd find a murky underground where what appears to be dissolves and mutates.

Beneath the parliament, the rats; beneath the hospital, the plague – all sealed up in catacombs of corpses and grim bones.

Beneath suburban gardens moan the slaves whose wretched lives are sacrificed for luxury and puff.

Beneath the clatter of the cutlery in restaurants and inns, the terror in the eyes of a thousand screaming beasts all bound for slaughter.

Beneath the banks, the sweatshops; beneath the schools,

the jails; beneath the shopping malls and their neon-lit deception seethes a pit of toxic waste. Beneath the words, the vacuum; beneath the name, conceit.

Yes – fall right through the mirage of mere death and find out just what it is that really strangles life! Will you dither endlessly, forever loudly claiming that you balance on the very brink?

Fall right down, if you dare... or merely slip, half-hearted and half-dead, along a gentler slope. Underwhelmed, you find it's more a mezzanine below, a parody of what you seek to flee.

Doors aplently lead into a hall that throbs with chat and fuss, a giant space through which great queues of people shuffle round. They disappear and then, at length, emerge to find the place where they began.

Oh, the satisfaction that this brings!

"We're back!" they shout "And now we plainly see how all ties in and forms a noose so tight to trap and bind!" They form themselves into small groups and pass again through passageways and loops – chanting as they go.

They think they've found the secret and that all they need to do is walk and walk all up and down and in and out until, by some strange spell, the tunnels will dissolve and rearrange into a nicer state.

Fools! Charlatans! Time wasters! Better they had stayed in bed than ambled in deluded bliss.

See there lurks a fine young man who hopes to find the proper way – and see his lip begin to curl at what plays out before his eyes. They wander in from here and there – good souls of all degree – only to be sent running as the unedifying unfolds clichés in abundance, self-righteous cant and disregard for others' thoughts and words.

Such are the tiresome traits that mark out those false prophets who block the way for others with true aim. Do not waste your time in here, I say – obey your heart and push right through and down!

Your heart – oh yes, that word I choose with some precision and yet it allows all manner of mistake. You might ask me how one can obey a thing of which one knows not where it lies – or when.

And as your prime exhibit you might present those episodes in which you led yourself so far astray in pursuit of what you felt to be its deepest wishes.

You look her in the eyes and are struck down silly by the radiance therein. And yet you know the shining of her soul is the glimmer in your own – a reflection and projection of that which we all share.

Pray pause a moment and assess the point in looking outwards for the truth that hides within. Release your heart from futile tasks and let it seek the secret of the sentient serene.

Down, you must go – down, down, down in pursuit of the Above. Shivers of self-doubt will keep shooting through your limbs and would nullify your efforts if you were foolish enough to give way to them.

I knew you of old. I know that you can reach out and touch the emptiness, absorb its pain and emerge still stronger than before. I know you can drive yourself ahead, cleanse yourself of the trivial and march out to meet fate head-on.

But I have also seen you fail at the very last, pull back from change that cannot be reversed, take fright at losing the little that you have for the being that you crave.

The fear has not left you – it is only held down. And at moments like this it emerges, dressed up as caution or restraint, and reveals all your fine courage to be fake.

I do not despise you for it. There is no intention to deceive in your incomplete resolve. But this is what I have come here for – to tell you to step out and leave your doubt behind.

If not, you are trapped forever in a stagnant pond of hopeless hope, all chocked up with knotted weeds of dreaming and delay. I have come to bid you deeper, so slip right through the crowd and walk past the doors all labelled and lit up.

Find your own way, my friend – wander as you would away from all the empty noise. Let disobedience be your code, as spelled out in your every step as serfdom is in others'.

Not just commands must be defied, but subtle guiles that steer you from your path and lead you into sinking sands. See through the lies! Attain the habit of refusal and resistance!

The shackles of conformity enslave us from within. Those petty rules, those stupid laws are made to wear you down. Thus you learn to go along, to toe the line and sing the song that others sing, to bow your head and stand in line and never question why.

Thus you lose connection to a sense of self and truth and confidence in what you see and know.

What's that you say? Ah, now, that's good – you challenge me for daring to dictate, for being just the outside force of which I seek to warn.

Know thyself is what I preach and nothing here will contradict that holy end. But, perhaps, your inner core lies deeper than you think and reaches wider than the consciousness by which you self-define...

Keep on down, my friend, and find your way by following the stench of what has been. A million years of falling from the truth, the whole, the light.

Disintegration hailed as multiplication – the numbers speak for themselves in the mathematics of the madhouse. Why enjoy the wood when there are so many trees to be counted and destroyed in the name of detail and deceit?

Who will stand up in the crawling crowd, look around and scream that all is lost? Who will risk the mockery of the maggot-mob, grow wings and smash his brains against the glass that hems us in?

To find freedom in the knowledge that we are not free, to find life within the ever-creeping shadow of impending death – this must be your task!

"Who do you think you are?" whine the slaves in great indignation and distress.

"What gives you the right to think you can throw off these chains that bind us all? Get yourself to work and then, like us, forget what you could be.

"Your talk of breaking out can only give offence to those who toil, heads down, and claim you as our own. We level-headed righteous folk will stay where we belong until the day we die, all poisoned and used up.

"What we don't see, does not exist. What we don't hear has made no sound. What we don't say cannot be said and what we do not understand must be destroyed!"

Flee! Turn on your heels and leave! There is nothing you can do for them right now. Run in here then clamber down into a whole new world.

Books. A hundred books on one long shelf. A thousand shelves in one huge room. A million rooms in just one wing. The library is of such a size you will never see it all, or even know how little you have seen.

There is, indeed, no need to visit more than one quite tiny part. In here you'll find a wealth of facts and thoughts and tales to fill your days. In here you'll find a refuge from the ignorance you fled, a ready source of nourishment for such a hungry mind. A trail of crumbs between the shelves, a feeling that there is a truth to be devoured.

See there on the wall hangs a clock with stealthy hands. Each time you turn away and read a page it rushes round towards the hour when little doors will part and, on a spring, a skull leaps out to yell "cuckoo!" and call an end.

So much to know, so much to learn – so swallow what you can then cast that book aside and live!

And now you're taking longer strides and feel the pace is picking up. A chasm opens up below. Leap now, leap! Fall now, fall! There is nothing in your way. Down and down, or up and up – it's hard to tell in darkness so complete your eyes are open wide and seem firm shut.

Into the mouth of the volcano must you tumble, losing all your fear in the roaring red rawness of this earthly womb. You land and find you're living still, and so much closer to your goal. But then you are waylaid.

A gentle murmuring drifts in through corridors obscure, all mingled with soft laughter so content. You move towards the source of such surprise – and find the wise ones, so passive and profound. They tell you that this cannot be, your mission now must end. There is no need, they say, to sink down to these depths, to force your route so far beneath the skin of all you know.

They smile and say they understand – they even may have once, long years ago, felt something of the same impulsive drive. But then they were naïve, then they were unformed, then they had not grown into a maturity so rich that black and white were both a nuanced grey.

"Congratulations", they smile. "Congratulations on arriving at our perfect point, so subtly poised between compliance and revolt. To muse, to mull, to modify – these are our high ideals. We make a difference – oh yes, we're held in high respect by those who mean to do the same as us.

"You, too, could join our clever cloud and float forever on the breezes of an self-regarding sky all curved round so slyly that you never realise you're trapped inside a giant sleepy sphere".

Turn your back and leave behind their polished walls of fraud to climb down to a darker place. Here crumbling stone and rotting wood frame dankness and the smell of tears.

Sense the screams of women burned a thousand years ago, the centuries of brutal primal force. Creep down between the flailing fists and cut-throat wiles, weave through the lynch mobs and the gangs of thieves whose sons are lords.

Descend the stairs that turn to rubble into a cave all stale and cold and still. Get on your knees and scrape away the blackened floor below. Broken nails are no excuse – dig harder with those dainty hands and tear apart this cake of cack.

Faster, further, until at last you strike the core, the thing itself beneath it all. Touch the walnut skin of this enormous cyst, this canker hardened by the wasting weight of time.

Hold your hand there on its shell and feel its evil throb. And then prepare yourself for what you have to do.

Breathe slowly and remember that this ever had to be. Stay silent for a moment, stay poised and calm inside. Then strike out with a vengeance at that which you despise!

Attack the seed of torment! Lash out for all you're worth! Fists and feet and elbows all must pummel at its bulk. Punch it, kick it, smash your skull against it and don't stop roaring your intent! Transform your hatred into waves of will that batter and beset!

Focus sharp and pierce its thickness with your cutting truth! Call up a resonance from around and shake its very structure with a rhythm that revolts! Throw yourself and all you are into the breaking of the beast! Rip yourself apart inside and hurl your bones and flesh in fury and despair!

Then just when you can do no more, a bolt of lightning, conjured up, cracks into the callus and – behold! – breaks it open and apart. A geyser of stinking pus! An eruption of black bloody bile!

And then a rumbling all around as cracks appear from underneath. Green shoots burst out! Tendrils and leaves and saplings and branches and then mighty oaks rise crashing through the shattered ground and grow on, grow up, breaking through the floors above as debris showers down.

Unblocked, unchained, a chaos of renewal as the life denied breaks out with energy unbound!

Rivers rise and flocks of birds and fish and bees and butterflies all swarm and float so free. Far above, a shaft of light as hope breaks out from underground and sunshine floods back in.

Now on the trees grow fruit and from the fruit spring children, all laughing at their birth. And you, my friend, have played your part.

You lie in pieces all around and in one sense you are no more. But at last you also know that you are me and we are all and this will always be.

THE POLITICS OF FEAR: TERRORISM AND STATE CONTROL

The fear of "terrorism" is an important tool for the plutofascist system in its attempts to intimidate its slaves and stop them from breaking free from exploitation and control.

But how would things look if we could show people that far from protecting them from some insidious threat, the system is itself that threat? How would things look if we could show them that the real terrorists are those in power?

This is not fanciful thinking – all we have to do is point people towards fully documented historical facts about the recent history of Europe.

After the end of the Second World War, the USA and UK secretly set up a network of "stay-behind" guerrilla units across western Europe, ostensibly to form a resistance movement in the event of a Soviet invasion. However, they quickly became part of efforts to keep radical movements from challenging capitalism and acted as terrorist cells, murdering hundreds of innocent people in a "strategy of tension" to scare the public into the arms of the state.

Gladio – as this network is known – is certainly not a widely acknowledged reality or a central part of the contemporary political background, but the facts have all been in the public sphere for some time now.

After many years of suspicions and rumours, initial confirmation of Gladio's existence came in Italy in 1974 as part of a probe into right-wing terrorism by investigative magistrate Giovanni Tamburino.

He arrested General Vito Miceli, chief of the Italian military secret service SID, on a charge of "promoting, setting up and organising, together with others, a secret association of military and civilians aimed at provoking an armed insurrection to bring about an illegal change in the constitution of the state and the form of government".

At his trial in November of that year, Miceli revealed the existence of a special section of SID, saying (in the words of this rather clumsy translation): "A Super SID on my orders! Of course! But I have not organised it myself to make a *coup d'état*. It was the United States and NATO who asked me to do it!".

And 16 years later, in 1990, an official confirmation came from Italian Prime Minister Giulio Andreotti, again as a result of Tamburino's investigations.

Andreotti revealed that, as far as Italy was concerned, a paramilitary movement had been set up immediately after the war and later formalised, in 1956, in a secret agreement between SIFAR (Italian military intelligence) and the CIA.

Says author Philip Willan, an expert in Italian political intrigue and author of a 1991 book on the subject: "Senior members of the network attended courses run by the Training Division of the British Intelligence Service. It was clear from the report that the organization had been in large part financed and controlled by the CIA".

On November 5, 1990, after Andreotti had already released details of Gladio, a NATO spokesman issued an official denial, stating firmly: "An organization of this kind does not and never has existed within the framework of the NATO military structure".

But the next day a different spokesman had to issue an

embarrassed retraction, saying the previous announcement had been "a mistake" and that NATO had no comment to make on the subject!

Shortly afterwards, the European Parliament passed a resolution condemning the network and saying it "protests vigorously at the assumption by certain US military personnel at SHAPE (Supreme Headquarters Allied Powers Europe) and in NATO of the right to encourage the establishment in Europe of a clandestine intelligence and operation network".

Obviously Andreotti and Italian president Francesco Corsica were not going to actually own up to any link between Gladio and terrorist attacks, but with connections already being made to the secret services, it did not take much of a leap of imagination to start to fill in the gaps and subsequent research and information leaves us with a pretty clear picture of what was going on.

Gladio's cover story of providing a "stay-behind" anti-Soviet network was undermined by the discovery of some of its 136 arms caches buried at secret locations around Italy. The weapons largely consisted of Kalashnikovs and other Soviet guns, plus explosives from Czechoslovakia (as it was). As Willan comments, why would the Americans and British go out of their way to supply groups with Eastern Bloc weapons if they were really intended to fight a Soviet invasion? The only obvious purpose is to use them to commit acts that can then be blamed on left-wing groups and the communist bloc.

In 1992 BBC2 screened a *Timewatch* documentary on Gladio by Allan Francovich, showing the close links between terrorists and western intelligence operatives. The film, *Operation Gladio*, can still, at the time of writing, be found on *YouTube* (see Endnotes).

The review in *The Times* at the time stated: "It was one of those programmes which you imagine will bring down governments, but such is the instant amnesia generated by television you find that in the newspapers the next morning it rates barely a mention".

Francovich went on in 1995 to make *The Maltese Double Cross* about the 1988 Lockerbie bombings. He died from a heart attack under mysterious circumstances upon entering the USA at the customs area of Houston, Texas, on April 17 1997.

Meanwhile, the investigations carried on, particularly in Italy. An Italian parliamentary commission into the country's years of terrorism concluded in 2000: "Those massacres, those bombs, those military actions had been organised or promoted or supported by men inside Italian state institutions and, as has been discovered more recently, by men linked to the structures of United States intelligence".

There were even confessions from the horse's mouth. In March 2001 General Giandelio Maletti, former head of Italian counter-intelligence, admitted: "The CIA, following the directives of its government, wanted to create an Italian nationalism capable of halting what it saw as a slide to the left and, for this purpose, it may have made use of right-wing terrorism".

The implications of all this are obviously enormous. As American author and intelligence analyst John Prados has commented: "In this age of global concern with terrorism, it is especially upsetting to discover that western Europe and the United States collaborated in creating networks that took up terrorism. In the United States such nations are called 'state sponsors' and are the object of hostility and sanction. Can it be the United States itself, Britain, France, Italy and others who should be on the list of state sponsors?"

Perhaps it is not so difficult to see why, despite the mountain of evidence on Gladio, it is still not widely mentioned in our media.

How did it all start? Well, dirty tricks go back a long way – from ancient Greece and Rome, through to the British Empire and the current day, all across the world and in all sorts of circumstances. The term "false flag", now often applied to terrorism carried out by someone other than it appears, originally came from a naval trick of attacking another force while flying the flags of an enemy, to prompt retaliation against the wrong target. Any power struggle or war has probably involved elements of deceit and manipulation.

But, for the purposes of this account, we will start the story at 9.15pm on the night of February 27, 1933, when a Berlin fire station received an alarm call that the Reichstag building, the home of the German Parliament, was ablaze.

The police quickly found a shirtless Dutch communist called Marinus van der Lubbe. He and four communist leaders were arrested and it was declared that the communists were beginning a plot against the German government.

Adolf Hitler, who had been sworn in as chancellor four weeks previously, urged President Hindenburg to pass an emergency decree in order to counter the "ruthless confrontation of the KPD". The passing of the Reichstag Fire Decree and then the Enabling Act led to the communists being barred from elections, various dissident papers being suppressed and generally allowed Hitler to take over the role of dictator.

In 1990 material from the Gestapo archives held in Moscow became available to researchers for the first time and a 2001 work by two German authors, Alexander Bahar and Wilfried Kugel, demonstrated that the fire was almost certainly started by the Nazis themselves.

We now jump across the North Sea and forward five years to 1938, when, with war with Germany looming, a report on guerrilla warfare by Major Lawrence Grand of the British army, suggested: "The use of organisations already existing in Germany, eg: the Communists". Using communists against fascists or fascists against communists – it was all fair game in British *Realpolitik*.

In 1939 Col Colin Gubbins produced some papers on guerrilla warfare. In *The Secret History of SOE – the Special*

Operations Executive, historian William Mackenzie notes: "In their final form, they consisted of three slender pamphlets printed on rice paper and bound in brown cardboard covers without indication of their contents.

"The original intention was to have them translated into various languages, but it is not at all clear what use was eventually made of them. They were entitled *The Art of Guerrilla Warfare* (22 pages), *Partisan Leader's Handbook* (40 pages) and *How to Use High Explosives* (16 pages plus diagrams)". Mackenzie writes of *The Art of Guerrilla Warfare*: "It is plain... that the doctrine is largely drawn from British experience in the offensive under Lawrence, on the defensive in Ireland, Palestine, the North-West Frontier and Russia".

By 1940, after Dunkirk, Britain was thinking as much about anti-Nazi resistance at home as on the continent. In May of that year Col Gubbins formed a new British resistance network to be supplied with the best weapons available and modern plastic explosives. It was highly secretive and its name, "Auxiliary Units", was chosen to be as nondescript as possible. It's still secret today, in fact, with official documents not to be released until 2020.

Author Daniele Ganser comments in his authoritative 2005 book *Nato's Secret Armies: Operation Gladio and Terrorism in Western Europe*: "These first British Gladio units received special training and were instructed to 'stay behind' enemy lines in case of a German invasion of the island. Operating from secret hideouts and arms caches, they would be able to carry out sabotage and guerrilla warfare against the German invaders".

Secret underground hideouts were set up all over England – *The Secret Sussex Resistance* by Stewart Angell (1996) describes some in Amberley and Arundel Park, with the local HQ at Tottington Manor in Small Dole, near Henfield. They contained arms to blow up railway lines and attack German army convoys plus 50-gallon oil drums filled with an inflammable mixture and buried in roadsides.

This is, in fact, pretty similar to the methods of the Iraqi and Afghan insurgencies against the US/UK occupations at the start of the 21st century. But, of course, such people are terrorists and our boys in the Second World War would have been resistance fighters, which is a completely different kettle of fish!

Britain was never invaded and so the stay-behind network was never activated. But the Germans left fascist stay-behinds as they withdrew across Europe to attack behind enemy lines, including the so-called Werewolves.

Experience from these paramilitary operations on both sides of the Second World War was to be used in the anti-communist struggle, with the "stay-behind" resistance networks set up supposedly in case of a Soviet invasion of American-controlled western Europe.

The Special Operations Executive had officially been disbanded in January 1946, but was secretly kept alive for the Cold War and on June 30 1947 a new "Special Operations" section was set up within MI6 under Gubbins. SOE personnel remained after the end of the war in Germany, Austria, Italy, Greece, Turkey and elsewhere as part of this new anti-communist operation, working closely alongside the Americans.

Gladio was first coordinated by the Clandestine Committee of the Western Union (CCWU), founded in 1948. After the creation of NATO in 1949, the CCWU was integrated into the Clandestine Planning Committee (CPC), founded in 1951 and overseen by the SHAPE (Supreme Headquarters Allied Powers Europe).

In Britain the Special Operations Executive – which had formed the wartime stay-behind units – was, naturally enough, involved. While the USA provided much of the funding for Gladio, Britain played a major role. There was a base near London and Gladio recruits trained with the SAS at Fort Monckton near Portsmouth, at Poole and also at Hereford –

home of the SAS.

What sort of people were recruited to become part of this pan-European network? Ganser, the author mentioned earlier, notes wryly that in Germany in 1945 "the supply of thoroughly anti-communist men trained in guerrilla warfare and experienced with arms and explosives was abundant". Former Nazis were used to set up a stay-behind network, including "Butcher of Lyon" Klaus Barbie and Hitler's spy chief Reinhard Gehlen. Elsewhere, fascist veterans of the Spanish Civil War, militants from Mussolini's last-stand Salo republic and other right-wing extremists were recruited and formed into squads of nine men, with two leaders. They were armed with light machine guns and hand grenades.

Similar networks were set up all across Europe, and we'll just briefly look at the sort of things they were up to before returning to the place where it all first went public – Italy.

SPAIN. Under Franco it has been said that Gladio was the actual government. CIA instructors trained European fascists in the Spanish Canary Islands. Parliamentarian Antonio Romera, of the Spanish United Left opposition party investigated and found Gladio in Spain had "acted against militant Communists and anarchists, such as against the miners of Asturias and the Catalan and Basque nationalists". In 1977, two years after Franco's death, a secret stay-behind army, with the support of Italian right-wing terrorists, carried out the Atocha Massacre in Madrid, attacking the offices of a lawyer connected to the Communist Party and killing five people.

PORTUGAL. A front organisation called Aginter Press was set up, backed by the CIA and used to recruit and direct fascists, backing Salazar's regime at home and in Portugal's African colonies. Anarchist Stuart Christie, in his book *Stefano della Chiaie*, says of Aginter Press's activities in the Portuguese African colonies: "Their aim included the liquidation of leaders of the liberation movements, infiltration, the installation of informers and provocateurs and the utilisation of false liberation movements". In Mozambique in 1969 Aginter Press assassinated Eduardo Mondlane, President of the Mozambique Liberation Party and leader of the FRELIMO movement. It is also believed that Portuguese and CIA agents from Aginter Press worked with Italian right-wing groups like Ordine Nuovo to plant bombs in Italy in 1969, which were blamed on left-wingers.

BELGIUM. In 1950 Gladio cells are thought to have been involved in the assassination of communist leader Julian Lahaut. In the 1980s, a horrific series of terrorist attacks was carried out, resulting in 28 deaths. Many suspect the Belgian branch of Gladio was involved. In an article in *The Observer* on June 7 1992, Hugh O'Shaughnessy wrote: "The objective of the exercise had been twofold: to jolt the Belgian police into a higher state of alert and, no less important, to give the impression to the population at large that the comfortable and well-fed Kingdom of Belgium was on the brink of red revolution".

GREECE. From the end of the war there was a long and bloody battle by Britain and the USA to keep the left out of power. When Greece joined NATO in 1952, the country's special forces, the LOK, were integrated into Gladio. Former Greek defence minister, Yannis Varvitsiotis has since admitted: "Local commandos and the CIA set up a branch of the network in 1955 to organise guerrilla resistance to any communist invader". In 1967 they were involved in a CIA-backed military coup one month before elections which the left was expected to win. This established the right-wing "Regime of the Colonels", which ran Greece until 1974.

TURKEY. The stay-behind army was known as "Counter-Guerrilla" and closely linked to the MIT, the Turkish intelligence agency. It was involved in domestic terrorism, killing hundreds of people as part of a "strategy of tension" that led to two military *coups d'état* in which it was directly involved – with secret American support – in 1971 and 1980.

NETHERLANDS. A Dutch section of the Gladio network, known as "O" and involved in top secret covert action and sabotage, was partly financed from private sources, it has emerged, particularly multinational firms.

NORWAY. The Norwegian stay-behind network defined its enemy of "fifth columnists" as "Norwegians or foreigners who, within the nation's borders, work for a foreign power through illegal intelligence activities, planning and carrying out sabotage, assassinations etc". Ironically, this is a perfect description of Gladio itself.

GERMANY. In the country where, you will recall, the network was set up with the help of senior Nazis, in 1981 a large stay-behind arsenal was discovered and linked to the bombing of the Munich October Beer Fest in 1980 that killed 13 and left 213 wounded.

Gladio has also been shown to have operated in France, Denmark, Austria, Finland, Sweden, Switzerland and Luxembourg.

ITALY. At the end of the Second World War, the American OSS, Office of Strategic Services – later to become the CIA – was at the head of the Allied wave invading Italy and the X2 counter-intelligence branch was charged with setting up a stay-behind network. Agent James Angleton deliberately recruited fascists, often saving them from execution by partisans out for revenge for atrocities committed against the local population.

The USA was desperate to keep the PCI – the communists – out of power in Italy. A cable sent in 1947 by George Kenna, director of the US State Department's Policy Planning Staff, stated: "As far as Europe is concerned, Italy is obviously key point. If communists were to win election there our whole position in the Mediterranean, and possibly in Western Europe as well, would probably be undermined".

CIA agent William Colby has said: "My job, simply put, was to prevent Italy from being taken over by the Communists in the next 1958 elections".

The USA was not too fussy about who it worked with to achieve its aims. It decided to use the mafia to rule southern Italy. Says Willan: "It was a natural choice, since Mussolini's ruthless crackdown on the criminal organizations meant the conservative-minded Mafia could be relied upon to be both anti-fascist and anti-communist".

The revival of Italy's Freemasons was also encouraged after the war by the UK and USA and the secretive and powerful P2 masonic lodge, under Licio Gelli, became a central point in the undercover battle to retain US/UK control of Italy. Silvio Berlusconi's name was among those found on a P2 membership list, and while P2 was supposedly banned in 1981, no doubt the same basic network still performs the same role today.

P2 membership included army officers, cops, judges and neo-fascists. Members boasted unswerving loyalty to anti-communism and American aims and policies in western Europe.

And for this role the Americans and British knew they could make good use of Italian fascists. An Ordine Nuovo document revealed in court in 1973 declared: "Behind the proud axe of Ordine Nuovo have gathered men who have no fear, whose violent force will descend implacably upon the filthy, bleating herd, led by Christian-Communist jackals". As Willan comments: "This is just the frame of mind required if one is to plant bombs in crowded public places".

Vincenzo Vinciguerra, a jailed neo-fascist bomber and Ordine Nuovo member who has spoken freely about the Gladio network, has said the "parallel structures" involving the intelligence forces were "an invisible army that is not poised for battle against a hypothetical invader, but rather one meant to be used internally".

The key to the Gladio approach in Italy was the "Strategy of Tension", designed to frighten the Italians into the arms of a right-wing state and thwart any radicalisation of Italian society.

The idea began at a Pollio Institute conference at the Parco dei Principe Hotel in Rome on May 3 to 5 1965, calling for all means possible to be used to defeat communism – secret service personnel, conservatives and fascists were involved.

In 1963 a secret NATO base was set up near Capo Marrargiu on the west coast of Sardinia which, it has now been officially admitted, was the official Gladio training centre. In 1968 it was expanded and modernised under the guidance of American "technicians". Its ostensible purpose was to train "stay-behind" units – supposedly to organise resistance and sabotage in case of a Soviet invasion of Italy. Says Willan: "More realistically, the units were to carry out sabotage and terrorism in peacetime Italy to ensure that Italian communists never got their hands on the levers of power".

In the decade from 1965 to 1975 between 1,000 and 4,000 potential terrorists were trained at the base. At the end of the course, Capo Marrargiu graduates would be allowed to keep the weapons and explosives with which they had been provided on arrival at the base.

The fascist Vinciguerra told the *Timewatch* documentary that he and other *Gladiatori* were transported to their training in Sardinia in blacked-out planes and buses and shown how to use explosives.

On December 12 1969 came the first major bombing of the Strategy of Tension in Italy at Piazza Fontana in Milan. 17 people killed and 88 injured. The attack was blamed on anarchists at the time. One of the suspects, Giuseppe "Pino" Pinelli, secretary of the Italian Anarchist Black Cross, died in police custody after being arrested and was the inspiration for Dario Fo's play *Accidental Death of an Anarchist*.

But in 1976, General Giandelio Maletti and Captain Antonio Labruna, both of the SID counter-espionage department, were arrested by magistrates investigating the bombing and accused of protecting suspects.

One of these, a right-winger by the name of Marco Pozzan, had been hidden in a secret service office for several days, supplied with a false passport and escorted to safety in Franco's Spain by a secret service officer.

Eventually, 17 years after the bombing, General Maletti was sentenced to a year in jail and Captain Labruna to ten months for their part in what was described in the charge as "a wider criminal plan aimed at preventing the judicial authorities from throwing light on the tragic terrorist events which bloodied Italy in 1969".

The pattern repeats over years of the Strategy of Tension, with official secrecy invoked to block investigations into terrorist acts. In 1989, in a speech marking the 20th anniversary of Piazza Fontana, Libero Gualtieri – a Republican Party senator and the president of an Italian parliamentary committee investigating the right-wing bomb massacres – said the judiciary had identified at least 40 instances of collusion between the secret services and right-wing terrorists.

Some fascinating documents, dated May 4 1969 (seven months before the Piazza Fontana bomb), were uncovered in 1971. They belonged to right-wing bombing suspect Giovanni Ventura and appeared to be reports drawn up for Italian secret services. One referred to a number of detailed steps to be taken towards moving the Italian government to the right, including "a possible wave of terrorist attacks to convince public opinion of the dangers of maintaining the alliance with the left (industrial groups in northern Italy would finance the planting of a few bombs by isolated neo-fascist groups)".

On May 17, 1973 Gianfranco Bertoli threw a hand grenade into a crowd outside the Milan police HQ, killing four people. He said he was an anarchist, but it later emerged he had worked for SIFAR (military intelligence) as well as for the right-wing CIA-Funded Peace and Freedom Association.

Mysterious deaths of witnesses were strangely frequent:

* Ermanno Buzzi, a right-wing bomber who was expected to make sensational revelations in court, was strangled in the corner of a prison yard by two right-wingers, Mario Tuti and Pierluigi Concutelli, on April 13, 1981.

* Carmine Palladino, thought to have inside info about the Bologna bombing, was murdered by Concutelli in the same corner of the same yard just over a year later, on August 10 1982.

* Pierluigi Paglia, a right-winger, who decided to return from Bolivia to tell magistrates what he knew about fascist bombings, was arrested in a joint CIA/Italian secret service operation and fatally wounded while allegedly resisting arrest on October 10 1988.

Probably the most notorious terrorist outrage in Italy took place on the morning of August 2, 1980, when a bomb at Bologna's main railway station killed 85 people and wounded more than 200.

It's common knowledge now that right-wing terrorists were to blame, and after lengthy investigations and countless court cases, in November 1995 (15 years later), the Court of Cassation (Corte di Cassazione) confirmed life imprisonment for the neo-fascists Valerio Fioravanti and Francesca Mambro, members of the Nuclei Armati Rivoluzionari (NAR).

But perhaps less well known is that sentences for "investigation diversion" – blocking the inquiry – were given by the same court to Licio Gelli (head of P2), and to secret service agents Francesco Pazienza, Pietro Musumeci and Giuseppe Belmonte.

Vinciguerra, the talkative fascist, told the *Timewatch* documentary: "The massacre at Bologna came at a time of maximum concern on the part of the Italian, American and Allied secret services because of the electoral success of the Italian Communist Party. The massacre at Bologna responds, as do all the other massacres, to the logic of a state which, no longer knowing how to confront a political enemy, resorts to extreme measures of violence, attributable to extremists, on the left or the right, in order to justify its own actions. That is the only truth about Bologna".

Another key event in recent Italian history was the kidnap and murder in 1978 of Christian Democrat leader and former Prime Minister Aldo Moro.

The one big difference between this and the other terrorist act we've mentioned so far is that it was carried out not by fascists, or fascists pretending to be anarchists or communists, but by the Red Brigades.

While nobody is suggesting that the Red Brigades were the total invention of the Italian state or the Gladio network, in the way that some of the neo-fascist groups undoubtedly were, there is much evidence to suggest that they were at least heavily infiltrated and probably even eventually secretly controlled by state forces.

An Italian intelligence officer has said the Red Brigades could be divided into three levels – the young fanatics, the Eastern Bloc agents and "further in, in the most secret compartment, the infiltrators of the Interior Ministry and Western secret services".

One strange piece in the jigsaw puzzle is a photocopier sold off as unserviceable from the Rome administrative office for the Gladio training base on Sardinia, which later appeared in perfect working order in the Red Brigades' printing shop in Via Pio Foa.

Left-wing terrorists sometimes chose some strange targets. For instance, in 1979 Prima Linea (Front Line), shot dead examining magistrate Emilio Alessandri, who was best known for his investigations into secret service involvement in right wing terrorism and who had just begun a probe into Banco Ambrosiano, the Milan bank headed by P2 member Roberto Calvi.

The change in the Red Brigades from its original relatively mild and idealistic nature to the violence of its later incarnation came in 1974 with the arrest of Renato Curcio and Alberto Franceschini, two of the founding fathers.

As author Gianfranco Sanguinetti has pointed out, nothing is easier for the secret services than to infiltrate a terrorist group and supplant the original leadership "either through certain timely arrests or through the killing of the original leaders, which generally occurs in a shoot-out with the police, prepared for the operation by their infiltrators".

Franceschini himself, one of the two arrested Red Brigades founders, had time in jail to work out what exactly he had been caught up in. He said: "We were the only revolutionary organization in an advanced capitalist country that had lasted over the years. I used to think that this meant that Italy was a country ripe for revolution... I had the impression that the *carabinieri* could have arrested us whenever they wanted, but they never went the whole way. Our activities were destabilising; those who used us did so in order to achieve a stabilizing effect, so that there should be no change to Italy, to maintain the exclusion from power of the Communist Party and of the left. We were acting to bring about change and those who used us did so to prevent change".

The kidnapping of Moro in particular has raised many questions about the Red Brigades. He was conveniently removed from the political scene while he was pursuing a policy of alliance with the Communist Party – a policy opposed by the P2 masonic lodge and the US government. He was kidnapped in a textbook operation on March 16. Two days later, an unnamed secret service officer told *La Repubblica* newspaper that the kidnap operation was a technical jewel, "so perfect as to seem almost artistic". He said it had to have been carried out either by highly trained soldiers or civilians "who have undergone lengthy commando training in specialized bases". He also referred to the Red Brigades' "genuinely ideologically motivated members" and "sectors that are controlled by other directors, for other purposes", commenting that their short-term aims "paradoxically coincide".

During his 55 days in captivity, Moro is said to have experienced the "Stockholm syndrome" of empathy with his kidnappers, and gave his captors controversial written confessions about the Strategy of Tension including, allegedly, the existence of Gladio. Bizarrely, his Red Brigade captors decided not to do anything with the material and, equally bizarrely, the Italian authorities declined to come to an agreement which would have led to his release – as they often did with much less prominent kidnap victims. On May 9 he was found dead in the boot of an abandoned car.

Moro's daughter Maria Fida, later a Christian Democrat senator, said: "Absolutely nothing was done. There were no negotiations; various attempts to negotiate were nipped in the bud".

Journalist Mino Pecorelli was amassing information on the Moro case and an unpublished article concerned speculation that the Americans were behind the kidnapping. He was shot dead in his car outside his office in March 1979. Pecorelli's friend Colonel Antonio Varisco of the *carabinieri* was murdered with a sawn-off shotgun in July 1979 and his colleague Captain Antonio Straullu, who investigated Pecorelli's death, was also assassinated.

While the USA has now admitted the existence of Operation Gladio, it insists it was merely a stay-behind network and, not surprisingly, denies it was involved in terrorist attacks in Italy and elsewhere.

But all the evidence points to heavy American involvement. This wasn't always necessarily the CIA, by the way. It was not always right tool for covert actions in Europe. There was the threat of exposure and thus an own goal in the sensitive game of US involvement in European politics. It is believed the FBI might have often been involved, even though – or rather because! – it ostensibly only operated on home soil. But the US also used other secret networks and channels –

parallel structures that did not show up on official paperwork.

As well as the statements linking the USA to Italian terrorism cited at the start of the talk, various other clues have cropped up over the years. For instance, a document confiscated from a plotter in a failed 1974 *coup d'état*, said the (proposed) new government's policies would include "maintenance of the present military and financial commitments to NATO and the preparation of a plan to increase Italy's contribution to the Atlantic Alliance" and the appointment of a special envoy to the USA to organise an Italian military contribution to the Vietnam war.

In 1981 top secret American documents were found in the false bottom of a suitcase being carried by the daughter of P2 boss Licio Gelli. These describe how US Army intelligence operatives should respond to communist insurgencies in Allied countries. One section warns that HC – Host Country – governments may be lulled into a false sense of security if the communist threat seems to have subsided: "In such cases, US Army intelligence must have the means of launching special operations which will convince HC governments and public opinion of the reality of the insurgent danger and of the necessity of counteraction. To this end, US Army Intelligence should seek to penetrate the insurgency by means of agents on special assignment, with the task of forming special action groups among the more radical elements of the insurgency. When the kind of situation envisaged above arises, these groups, acting under US Army intelligence control, should be used to launch violent or non-violent actions according to the nature of the case".

Willan concludes: "It is by no means easy to determine who was responsible for day-to-day tactical decisions in the running of the strategy of tension. But there can be little doubt that overall responsibility for the strategy lay with the government and intelligence services of the United States".

But it would be wrong to think that the USA is the only

state heavily implicated in Gladio and officially sanctioned terrorism. And also wrong to think that the waves of terror that hit Italy were the worst in Europe.

In Italy, between 1969 and 1987, 365 people were killed and more than 1,000 wounded in political violence.

But during the same years in another part of Europe, 2,618 were killed and more than 33,000 injured. Where was that nightmarish place? Northern Ireland. And what is the state often accused of involvement in the violence? Britain.

We can't do anything more here than scratch the surface of the history of the troubles, but if we could, we might want to look more closely at:

* Freddie Scappaticci, alias Stakeknife, the British agent who infiltrated the IRA to run its internal security and ordered 40 people to be murdered as security risks – presumably the wrong ones. He's now said to be living in Italy, where he no doubt feels very much at home.

* Brian Nelson, the British agent who became the intelligence chief of the loyalist Ulster Defence Association – performing a similar role on the other side of the deadly maze of mirrors.

* The Birmingham Six, Guildford Four, and the Maguire Seven – all people wrongly convicted of republican bombing atrocities. Or maybe we should put some inverted commas around "republican", because if they're not responsible, who knows who was really behind the outrages and why the British establishment was so keen to find someone to blame for them. Incidentally, the Birmingham bomb led to the 1974 Labour government passing the original Prevention of Terrorism Act.

* Question marks remain over the Omagh bombing of August 15 1998, generally blamed on a republican splinter group. Suspicious minds have pointed to the fact that public horror at the attack, in which 29 people died, allowed Tony Blair's government to rush through controversial "emergency" anti-terrorist legislation, in the form of the Criminal Justice

(Terrorism and Conspiracy) Act 1998, less than a month later in September 1998. This allowed people to be convicted of belonging to a proscribed organisation merely on the say-so of a senior police officer, created an offence of conspiracy to commit offences abroad and generally prefigured more recent terrorist legislation. Helpfully, it included a clause giving "all crown agents immunity from prosecution under the legislation".

* Constant suspicions of the involvement of the British state in sectarian killings, which still won't go away, even though its focus switched suddenly to a new "war on terror" just as the "troubles" were declared over. Questions have been asked about state involvement in the deaths of Rosemary Nelson, loyalist Billy "King Rat" Wright, catholic Robert Hamill and RUC officers Harry Breen and Bob Buchanan.

In 2012 Prime Minister David Cameron was forced to admit that the level of state collusion uncovered by a report into the murder of Belfast solicitor Pat Finucane was "shocking" – though the report predictably concluded there had been "no overarching state conspiracy". No, of course not.

There is an overspill into mainland politics as well, with researcher Larry O'Hara, for example, pointing to a state agenda to reflect the IRA/Loyalist battleground with an anti-fascist/extreme-right conflict in England, by use of infiltrators, agents provocateurs and pseudo-gangs. The 1999 nail bombings bombings in London, supposedly carried out alone and unaided by a right-wing extremist David Copeland, come under some suspicion, not least because the authorities seem to have known, in advance, exactly what area he would target with his final bomb.

There are, of course, continuing questions marks over recent "Islamic" terrorist attacks, with theories abounding over who was really responsible for 9/11 or 7/7 and attention drawn to the links between British and American intelligence services, Pakistani intelligence services and groups like Al Quaeda – suddenly on "our side" in Syria.

One state organisation heavily involved in the dirty war in Ireland was the SAS. Glorified by the right-wing media, this elite and secretive branch of the military is in fact more or less Britain's answer to the SS.

Formed in 1942 to strike behind enemy lines in North Africa, it was disbanded at the end of the war in October 1945, its job apparently over. Adds Ganser in his book on Gladio: "Yet as the need for top-secret dirty tricks and daredevil operation resurfaced as quickly as the global power of the British Empire was declining, the SAS was reborn and in 1947 fought behind enemy lines in Malaysia".

Since then, the SAS has remained at the forefront of British imperialism – it stormed the Iranian embassy in 1980, fought in the Falklands War in 1982, the First Gulf War in 1991, and secretly trained and equipped Kosovo Liberation Army forces in 1999, in close liaison with their friends in the US Green Berets, a kind of transatlantic twin organisation. In 1990 a BBC documentary called *The Unleashing of Evil* revealed how the SAS and the Green Berets had used torture against prisoners over the past 30 years and in every major campaign from Kenya to Northern Ireland, Oman, Vietnam, Yemen and Cyprus. The SAS and Green Berets trained Khmer Rouge units in Cambodia under Thatcher and Reagan and the SAS trained the Mujahedin, future Al Quaeda and Taliban fighters, in bomb-making and other black arts in Pakistan in the 1980s and 1990s, as revealed by John Pilger in his book *The New Rulers of the World*.

Current SAS roles are said to include "Counter Terrorism operations inside and outside UK territory; training soldiers of other nations, and training guerrillas in unconventional warfare and counter revolutionary warfare activities in support of UK government Foreign Policy".

As mentioned earlier, the SAS was definitely involved in Gladio, acting as the training arm for guerrilla warfare and sabotage. Italian stay-behind units were trained in Britain and the SAS built secret hides where arms were stashed in West Germany. They also collaborated closely with an armed undercover Swiss organisation called P26. They offered training in Britain, with the SAS also visiting Switzerland. The Swiss even took part in a real assault on an IRA arms depot in which at least one IRA activist was killed, reveals Ganser.

This insidious role carries on today. Take Simon Mann, the supposedly "former" SAS man who has admitted being involved in an attempted *coup d'état* in Equatorial Guinea, along with the late Margaret Thatcher's son Mark.

Or Ben Griffin, the ex-SAS soldier who spoke at a Stop the War press conference in 2008 about Britain's role in illegally kidnapping people and handing them over to be tortured and was promptly served with a gagging injunction by the British government.

It is sometimes too easy to focus on American atrocities across the world, from Latin American coups to Vietnam or Guantanamo Bay, and turn a conveniently blind eye to the role our own state has played and still is playing, as the USA's number one partner in crime.

Historian Mark Curtis wrote in *Web of Deceit* in 2003: "The idea that Britain is a supporter of terrorism is an oxymoron in the mainstream political culture, as ridiculous as suggesting that Tony Blair should be indicted for war crimes. Yet state-sponsored terrorism is by far the most serious category of terrorism in the world today, responsible for far more deaths in many more countries than the 'private' terrorism of groups like Al Quaeda. Many of the worst offenders are key British allies. Indeed, by any rational consideration, Britain is one of the leading supporters of terrorism in the world today. But this simple fact is never mentioned in the mainstream political culture".

So what lessons can we learn from all this?

Firstly, it is important to acknowledge that there does exist a powerful capitalist military-industrial complex, which is completely ruthless in pursuing its aims. It's clear that it is not specifically communism that is the enemy of this system – though during the Cold War and specifically in Italy the communists were seen as the main threat – but anything that threatens to block the domination of certain commercial interests. Curtis has written of "Britain's overwhelming need to keep economic resources in the correct hands – élites who give favourable treatment to western business".

In his 1988 book *The Culture of Terrorism*, Noam Chomsky recalls how, in the Second World War, US president Franklin Roosevelt had announced the Four Freedoms that the US and its allies would uphold in the conflict with fascism: freedom of speech, freedom of worship, freedom from want and freedom from fear. Says Chomsky: "The central – and not very surprising – conclusion that emerges from the documentary and historical record is that US international and security policy, rooted in the structure of power in the domestic society, has as its primary goal the preservation of what we might call 'the Fifth Freedom', understood crudely but with a fair degree of accuracy as the freedom to rob, to exploit and to dominate, to undertake any course of action to ensure that existing privilege is protected and advanced".

It's not just through terrorism or repression that this global control is maintained – there is a whole spectrum of activities ranging from the funding of political parties and the grooming of up and coming politicians, through to the control of the media. We have to acknowledge this as a reality and direct our efforts accordingly. For instance, if this system is ruthless enough to commit acts of terrorism on its own public, or stage *coups d' état* to preserve its total grip on power, can anyone really believe it would allow a radical group to take that power away from it by winning an election?

It's just not going to happen, any more than genuine radical groups are currently going to be able to seize control of the state through an armed revolution. There's no point in fighting the state on a terrain on which it is bound to win. We have to look first at more subtle, unstructured, chaotic, organic, subversive methods of bringing about change and winning our freedom, working through flexible protest and direct action, grassroots community activity, alternative media – creating our own parallel structures, if you like.

Secondly, the police spy revelations in the UK media in 2013 hopefully mean that more people realise that state infiltrators and agents provocateurs are not a paranoid invention and do really exist. But we should also be aware that what we know can only be the tip of the iceberg and that the role of state spies is not just to watch or sabotage but also to control the direction groups take.

We should also note that the state's efforts are particularly successful where there exists an organisational hierarchy which they can take over. Gianfranco Sanguinetti, in his book *Of Terrorism and of the State*, argues it is easy for secret services to take control of genuine groups and manipulate them to their own advantage: "All secret terrorist groups are organized and run by a hierarchy which is kept secret even from their own members, and which reflects the division of labour typical of this kind of social organization: decisions are taken at the top and carried out by the bottom. Ideology and military discipline protect the true leaders from any risk and the base from any suspicion".

Obviously this doesn't just apply to paramilitary groups, but any radical movement. Everyone has a responsibility to think for themselves. If you don't follow orders, you can't be used for someone else's purposes. It's no coincidence that it is fascist and communist groups – both very hierarchical in outlook – that were successfully hijacked for state purposes.

Thirdly, it is clearly important that we should not allow ourselves to be mentally manipulated by terrorism. The head of steam that had been built up by the anti-capitalist movement in the USA, after Seattle and so on, was pretty much dissipated by 9/11 – an example of the *Shock Doctrine* set out by Naomi Klein in her well-known book. That wave of dissent didn't really swell up again until the Occupy movement. Anyone active in radical politics around that time will recall meeting people after the Twin Towers bombing who were saying the world had changed completely now and they couldn't carry on protesting. On 7/7 at the Stirling camp for the 2005 G8 protests, news came through of the London bombings. Immediately a resolution was proposed, and somehow passed by a system of delegate voting, declaring that in the circumstances "confrontational" protest was no longer appropriate...

We should also learn to tell the difference between armed resistance and terrorism – globally as well as domestically – and be able to spot the possible motivation behind attacks.

Ganser writes that the Rote Armee Fraktion and the Red Brigades (although they were eventually both infiltrated) "did not attack mass gatherings of the population, but very selectively targeted individuals whom they thought represented the 'state apparatus', such as bankers, generals and ministers whom they kidnapped and often assassinated... Contrary to the terror of the left, the terror of the right aimed to strike fear to the bones of the entire society and hence secretly planted its bombs among the population to kill large numbers indiscriminately in order to wrongly blame the Communists".

Said the fascist Vinciguerra: "You had to attack civilians, the people, women, children, innocent people far removed from any political game. The reason was quite simple. They were supposed to force these people, the Italian public, to turn to the State to ask for greater security. This is the political logic that lies behind all the massacres and bombings which remain unpunished, because the state cannot convict itself or declare itself responsible for what happened".

Ultimately, the most important weapon in our armoury is

information. We should spread knowledge of how the state operates, of the fact that it has used terrorism as a device for its own ends in the past and may well do so again.

This is not the same as automatically assuming that every terrorist attack that happens is a fake – that won't always be the case. But by studying examples from the past and taking the patterns that they tend to follow, we can get a fairly good idea of what is likely to be going on and inform other people of this.

The whole point of state terror is to trick the population into reacting in the way that the state desires. If the powers-that-be know that nobody is falling for it any more, there will be no point in them using the strategy in the first place.

LI AND THE ORGANIC FREEDOM OF ANARCHY

It may only consist of two letters in our alphabet, but the Chinese term *li* strikes me as being particularly important for anarchism. Alan Watts says as much, in fact, in his book *Tao: The Watercourse Way*, when he describes the concept around *li* as "analagous to Kropotkin's anarchy".[1]

Li is all about natural order, an innate and organic pattern to life that emerges without external control or direction. Watts explains: "Though the Tao is *wu-tse* (nonlaw), it has an order or pattern which can be recognized clearly... This kind of order is the principle of *li*, a word which has the original sense of such patterns as the markings in jade or the grain in wood. *Li* may therefore be understood as organic order, as distinct from mechanical or legal order, both of which go by the book. *Li* is the asymmetrical, nonrepetitive, and unregimented order which we find in the patterns of moving water, the forms of trees and clouds, of frost crystals on the window, or the scattering of pebbles on beach sand".[2]

He adds: "If each thing follows its own *li* it will harmonize with all other things following theirs, not by reason of rule imposed from above but by their mutual resonance (*ying*) and interdependence".[3]

This concept of organic order is an essential part of the

anarchist vision. This is why anarchists don't accept that we need a state or other form of top-down control to regulate human society – we believe our society can regulate itself, from within and from below, in the same way as other parts of the natural world.

It is also the reason why anarchists don't generally provide a detailed blueprint for the society we would like to see replace the current industrial-capitalist nightmare. It is no more for us to say what this *ought* to be like, than it is for anyone else.

If we really believe in anarchy, in organic democracy, then we can do little more than talk about the kind of way we would imagine people living when freed from the yoke of authority. There certainly can be no question of planning, let alone compulsion.

In order to be comfortable with this position, we need to have complete faith in humanity, we need to believe that, while there will always be problems and conflicts within communities, a critical mass of people are sociable, well-meaning, caring, inventive, courageous or diligent individuals who will naturally come together to form a coherent and healthy society. Our *ying*, our mutual resonance and interdependence, will ensure that this happens.

The task before us, therefore, is to clear the blockage created by modern civilization and its mindset and thus allow us to rediscover our natural freedom in the invisible and indescribable *li*.

TRANSCENDENT ANARCHY

June Singer's *Boundaries of the Soul: The Practice of Jung's Psychology,* first published 40 years ago, makes for very interesting reading and one particular section suggests strong parallels with the psychology of anarchism.

Note that this is not an attempt to devalue the significance of the individuation process on a personal level or to relate Singer's work purely to certain political interests in some glib and superficial manner!

Indeed, the processes that lead to inner realisation and wholeness are as important for an anarchist as the external action that he or she undertakes.

There would be nothing strange in this thought for Carl Jung, immersed as he was in the alchemical tradition of microcosm and macrocosm, of correspondences between all levels of existence.

Anyway, the paragraph that first leads us in that direction is concerned with the reasons for which an individual develops a neurosis. Singer explains that it is not some kind of random mental fault, but that there is a purpose behind it.

She writes: "This involves correction of some conscious attitude that prevents the individual from more fully realizing his total capacity. When normal productive means of achieving one's purpose are blocked off, neurosis develops as an effort to find a way over or around the obstruction".[1]

This echoes the metaphor of "antibodies" being activated to fight off the mental disease currently affecting humanity. When the natural self-correcting processes of society are blocked – by all the levels of repression and control that protect the status quo – then a neurosis develops as an "an effort to find a way over or around the obstruction".

Those who look aghast at the confrontational approach recommended by anarchists have failed to understand its context. While the society to which anarchists look forward is peaceable and co-operative (unlike the current so-called "order" which has to be imposed by violent force), the path to that society is blocked and the only way to breach the block is to temporarily assume a more pro-active form.

This urgent need for action on the social level is reflected in Singer's description of the individual process, when she says there is no time for self-pity or regrets and that "today we know what our task is and, therefore, today we must address ourselves to it".[2]

She writes that much individual emotional disturbance is due to "a lack of correspondence between the conscious orientation and the unconscious purposes"[3] and we could continue the parallel on to the macrocosmic social level.

Millions of people today simply cannot cope with living in the modern world, in which our lives are so denuded of meaning. Increasing numbers take anti-depressants, others take to drink or drugs, most somehow numb themselves to a wider external reality that is too depressing or frightening to really think about. The buried awareness of our plight is our shared unconscious.

Meanwhile, at the same time, we are offered no alternative to this world. The confines of permissible thought are drawn tightly around variations on the same capitalist, industrialist, materialist theme. Anything else is derided as laughable, unrealistic or dangerous. This, on a political level, is our conscious orientation.

With an unconscious rejection of the modern world and a conscious commitment to preserving it, there is clearly a significant lack of correspondence between the two levels, leading to social neurosis.

The answer on an individual level, says Singer, is a third element called "the transcendent function", which belongs neither to the ego sphere nor to the unconscious, and yet possesses access to each.

"It stands above them, participating in both. It is as though ego and unconscious were points at either end of the baseline of a triangle. The third element, at the apex of the triangle, transcends both the point of the ego and the point of the unconscious but is related to each of them. The transcendent function's emergence grants autonomy to the ego and also to the unconscious by relating to both of them independently, and in doing so, unites them".[4]

This, on the larger scale, is the transcendent function of anarchy. Rooted in the collective unconscious of humanity, it is connected to the conscious political sphere but does not fully belong to it. The task for anarchism is to transcend the other two elements and thereby to unite them.

We must bring out the loathing of the capitalist-industrialist world that bubbles up in the unconscious soul of humanity and incorporate it into the realm of reality, of politics if you like, so that the neurosis of modernity can fulfil its purpose of freeing us from the prison of this civilization and allowing us to live naturally to our fullest and healthiest "total capacity".

PAUL CUDENEC

FIGHTING CAPITALISM ON EVERY LEVEL

There is a certain current of anarchist thinking that is very particular about the way we perceive and define capitalism.

It takes special affront at propaganda that identifies capitalism with specific institutions or events, such as banks or the latest summit. Capitalism, this current points out, is a matrix of economic and social relationships and not simply this or that building or group of people.

There is obviously some truth in this analysis and it would be dangerously superficial to focus exclusively on the public faces of capitalism without attempting any analysis of what it is, where it comes from and how it might be defeated rather than merely symbolically challenged.

However, this criticism – usually aimed at attempts to organise populist mass street action – is fundamentally flawed and wilfully ignores the fact that capitalism exists on many different levels and should therefore also be countered on many different levels.

In its most disembodied form, we might see "capitalism" as nothing but a word, consisting of the shape of the letters that spell it out. Next, in order of descent towards the tangible, it is an abstract definition which would exist even if there were no capitalist societies anywhere on the planet (as was once the case and surely will be again!).

This is one of the levels that these particular critics tend to focus on, along with the next one down, which is the capitalist system actually in place, as it is in our times, with all the complexities it involves.

An important part of any anti-capitalist struggle will always be the analysis and description of capitalism, in theory and in practice, and the discussion of alternatives – this is not something that would be disputed by anyone.

But capitalism also exists on less abstract levels of reality. It manifests itself in the real world in the shape of real companies which have real headquarters and are run by real people.

It also manifests itself in the form of the politicians who maintain its hegemony, and most noticeably when these politicians, heads of various capitalist states, come together publicly to present a common front at the various summits that are essentially propaganda initiatives on behalf of the status quo.

Opposing these manifestations of capitalism does not necessarily mean one has no understanding of the less tangible forms that capitalism takes, or that one mistakes buildings or men in suits for the phenomenon that we term capitalism.

Instead, protesters in the financial districts of London or outside a summit are choosing to counter capitalism on the levels at which it becomes obviously visible, deploying their own symbolism of protest and dissent against its equivalent symbols of power and control.

The same multi-layered reality applies to any political ideology or system. Fascism, for example, is also a word in the dictionary. It is also a political theory of sorts (though a rather incoherent one) and it has been, historically, a real form of social organisation and control.

Fascism was never exactly the *same thing* as the German or Italian governments in the 1930s, but it *manifested* itself, in a less pure and more worldly form, in those governments.

Fascism as a concept is not the *same* as the actual existing

Golden Dawn party in Greece or the EDL or BNP in the UK, but it *manifests* itself in those organisations.

Would any anarchist ever argue that there is no point in protesting outside the HQ of one of these fascistic organisations, or in mobilising against their marches or rallies, on the basis that fascism is a system rather than a building or an event? Is there any anarchist who would not understand that we have to be present on the same levels as fascism is present, in order to oppose it in whatever form it appears?

Again, if we lost track of the bigger picture and fixated on specific individuals or groups without understanding the context in which they arose, there would be ground for criticism, but this is not an inevitable by-product of choosing to challenge fascism in a specific manifestation.

Likewise, mobilising against bankers or summits under the banner of anti-capitalism does not inevitably involve any lack of understanding of what capitalism is nor, indeed, preclude involvement in the struggle against capitalism on other levels, whether more abstract or more pragmatic.

The kind of analysis that is forever positing an "either/or" scenario (and of course insisting that its particular approach is the correct one!) does nothing to further the cause of anarchism. Ours must be a holistic approach, operating simultaneously in microcosm and macrocosm, understanding that just as capitalism manifests in both abstract and tangible forms, so must we.

"We are everywhere" has a broader application than the merely geographic.

PAUL CUDENEC

TOWARDS THE END OF THE WEEK:
THE TYRANNY OF TIME

Some of the units we use to measure time just can't be argued with. The spinning of the earth or its orbit around the sun are clear reasons for the existence of a "day" or a "year" — and even a month is more or less in tune with lunar reality. But the same just can't be said for a "week", an oddity of which the origins and purpose are obscure.

The biblical reference to the "seventh day" of rest does not mean that the seven-day week has been anything like universal over the centuries. The ancient Egyptians used a ten-day week and the Mayan calendar used a 13 and a 20-day period. Lithuanians used weeks of nine days before adopting Christianity. There's nothing natural about the week. It's an enclosure of time, an artificial construct imposed on the world by a succession of centralising, controlling forces from the Roman Empire, through the Christian Church and the British Empire to the global techno-business hegemony of today.

We have now reached the point where the seven-day week has completely enchained us to its rigid cycle of routine and the limited horizon with which it has been stifling humanity for far too long. When we wake up each morning, what we are really experiencing is a new day, a day we have never experienced before. But the first thought that enters our heads on regaining consciousness is whether this day is a "Monday", a "Saturday" or a "Thursday".

It seems that each of these days already has its own character before it has even unfolded. And yet what lies ahead of us in the future is in reality a series of unlived days which are but blank canvases on which we can paint our dreams and our lives. Instead of that, we see nothing but short, brutal closed loops of "days of the week", tired and familiar clichés through which we have trudged time and time again in our sadly confined lives.

This is of course ideal for those who would keep us as their slaves on a perpetual treadmill of production, for those who fear the moment we raise our gaze from the factory formula of routine and catch a glimpse of the free-time world which should have been our lifelong playground.

From early in life, children are taught to mould themselves into the authoritative contours of the official week. "Tuesday is painting day. Friday is dressing-up day".

When they start school, they are also forced to swallow the biggest lie of all — the weekend. The weekend is good, we are told. It is special. It is something to be celebrated. It is our freedom. And yet its true role is to confirm that the other five days of the week are set aside for slavery. By the time children come out of their educational processing, they no longer question this, no longer dare suggest that the finite days of their unique, precious, existence on this earth belong to them and to nobody else.

As would-be liberators of the human race, we must look beyond superficial changes in social organisation. We must dig deep to uproot the imagination of our species from the dank heavy sterility into which it has grown embedded.

We must not waste a single minute calling for shorter working hours or fewer working days. We must aim higher in our attack on temporal tyranny. It is time we looked as far ahead as the end of the week!

PLUTOFASCISM DEFINED

plutofascism (ˌplutə'fæʃɪzəm) n. 1. the rule or control of society by the wealthy by means of an authoritarian and hierarchical structure that is fundamentally opposed to democracy. 2. any ideology justifying the rule of the wealthy and the imposition of an authoritarian and hierarchical structure to maintain that rule.

AN INTERVIEW WITH PAUL CUDENEC

Q: Your book The Anarchist Revelation is very much focused around presenting an anarchist spirituality. Why?

That's the question I hopefully go some way to answering over the course of some 150 pages! In short, there are two separate, and yet interwoven, strands. Firstly there is the individual question – how can an alienated individual such as an anarchist, who is sane enough to find the contemporary capitalist world insane, carry on living in that world? Involvement in the anarchist struggle is part of the answer, but you also need something more than that, some greater perspective to fall back on in times of doubt or isolation.

I think anarchism, historically, has always offered a depth of vision that can sustain and propel an individual through adversity but, if we start to regard anarchism not as a life-philosophy but as a narrowly defined social movement, we will lose contact with that vital force.

Secondly, there's the spiritual depth of the anarchist movement as a whole. To me, it stands opposed to the modern materialist mindset at a fundamental level. It's not just that we reject all those assumptions about the legitimacy of authority, property or privilege, but we also reject the blinkered and one-dimensional thinking of the current age.

Anarchy is lateral thinking, creative thinking, poetic thinking in many ways, and in that it has a lot in common with something like Sufism, the esoteric strand of Islam. It's not stuck on the one level – like Marxism is, for example. And I think we need to reconnect to that imaginative and fluid side of anarchist thought.

Q: But there's a difference between the vitality or fluidity of a philosophy and this idea of "spirituality". Where does that come in? Why does it have to come in?

Spirituality for me is all about using the parts of our mind that are left to wither away in a purely materialist society, where nothing is considered valid unless it can be "empirically" proven to be so. These are the powers we need to reignite, on both an individual and collective level.

Q: But what about the religious aspect to "spirituality" that you do evoke in your book? Are you suggesting that these unused parts of our mind are something to do with a supernatural element?

Not supernatural, no. But my definition of what is natural, and real, would go a lot further than what's generally understood by that. As far as religion goes, the only religion I'm promoting is anarchism. OK, maybe it's not quite a religion at the moment, but I think it has the potential to be, if it doesn't cut itself off from the less materialist aspects of its philosophy that take it up in that direction.

Q: So what kind of religion would anarchism be? A religion with no god?

There doesn't have to be a "god", in the sense in which it's normally meant in the West. It's all about a holistic vision, understanding that on every level of existence everything is interconnected and ultimately part of the one entity. On a human level, this is already the anarchist position – mutual aid, co-operation, solidarity and so on. On a planetary level this is the environmentalist position – the Gaia idea of a living Earth. On a cosmic level, this becomes a Buddhist or Taoist idea of the ultimate unity.

I think that anarchism naturally embraces the holistic approach on the other levels, as well, thus expanding itself into a complete vision of life, rather than remaining merely a social or economic programme spiced up with a confrontational attitude.

Q: Is this a bad thing, then, a "confrontational attitude"? Should anarchists be adopting the quietism of Eastern mystics?

Not at all. A confrontational attitude is essential for anarchism. I think we need to be more confrontational, in fact, in contexts other than street battles with the police or fascists. We need to be more confrontational in our refusal of the moral claims of the state, by stating clearly that we don't accept that they have the right to rule us, to jail us, to control us in any way. Of course, we recognise the reality that they can do so, in the same way that a large man with a knife has the physical ability to rob me in the street, but we should make it clear that we don't buy into their lie that there is any moral legitimacy behind this.

We also need to be more confrontational in attacking the limits that are placed around possible futures. Although it's often a tactically good idea to work with reformist campaigns, if only to help stem the tide of increasing capitalist domination, we should never stop talking about the completely different society that is our vision and inspiration. It doesn't matter if people can't grasp that this could ever happen, that they are conditioned by society to think that such a future is not only undesirable but also impossible.

We have to keep our black flag flying so that the vision stays alive and it's there for people to turn to one day when they finally realise that the only alternative is going to be a future of slavery and misery for the vast majority of humanity. What we need to reclaim is the total opposition to the current system that was historically offered by anarchism. There's such a strength in that.

Also, by the way, there's nothing necessarily quietist or pacifist about faiths like Buddhism – take the Tibetan monks in their struggle against Chinese occupation, for a start. Many religions are used by authorities to promote obedience and submission, and Buddhism is no exception, but that doesn't reflect on its innate qualities or its potential as an aid to human liberation.

Q: Total opposition? That sounds quite full-on!

In the context in which I just used it, I meant total opposition in a philosophical sense – attacking the current death-system at its roots, rather than focusing on trimming it back here and there. But I do think that's what we need, at every level. Otherwise nothing will change, all possibilities of improvement will remain blocked and the future will be like this, only a thousand times worse.

Q: There's a strong environmental current running through your work. Would you describe yourself as an eco-anarchist?

I have done, yes, though I'm tending now to focus on just being an anarchist, which I think is enough. For a start, I can't see that anything other than anarchism – and the total opposition that it involves – is going to save the planet. The system is not going to reform itself or voluntarily concede any power or control.

I also don't feel there's a need for any of us to qualify our anarchism with adjectives. I've been playing around with the notion of an Anarchy Threshold, this being the "finishing tape" that all anarchists are aiming at, the point at which humankind can said to be liberated. The idea is that we don't really have to argue about what happens after that, because, as anarchists, we're saying that the people around at the time (whenever it actually happens!) will decide that, by their actions and views, among themselves.

So it doesn't matter if my vision of a better future is one without factories, while my comrade sees the need for a continuation of some form of industrialism. Neither of us will be in a position to decide that. As anarchists we're not about imposing our views on others anyway, even if we could do so. So it's purely theoretical – our only input is in putting forward our own visions of how life could be. If we have faith in a free humanity, we will have faith in the future it will create for itself in an anarchist society.

Personally, I can't see that a post-capitalist world would be industrial in any way, because industrialism is capitalism. The capitalists are right when they say that without the profit incentive, we wouldn't have what they call "progress" – it's the forces of money and power, feeding off each other, that have spawned the industrial hell in which we are all forced to live today and the moment that there is no more capitalism there will be no *raison d'être* for factories, oil refineries, nuclear power stations, shopping malls and so on.

I don't have to argue too much with other anarchists about what a future anarchist society would look like, though. Firstly, because it's not my call – or theirs. Secondly, because I know, in my own heart, that an anarchist society would not be an industrial one. It will all unfold in due course. And in the meantime, before the Anarchy Threshold has been reached, our only aim should be to work towards that point with a diversity of tactics and a respect for each others' personal visions.

Q: Isn't that a bit naïve, to think that anarchists could all work together happily ever after?

It's not naïve to think we *should* all work together – or at least not snipe at each other. If we can't, then perhaps that's something to do with the egos of individuals concerned (not just inflated egos, but fragile ones as well) – and that is something that can be addressed by an individual spiritual approach that is a microcosm of our social struggle, as I describe in the book. It's about rediscovering our strength and clarity, both individually and collectively.

Q: The language in your book can be quite academic at times – do you feel that this can create a barrier to people understanding what you're saying and limit the numbers who are going to read your message?

Firstly, I'm not a professional academic and I try to make my meaning clear to readers. It's difficult, though, to express complex ideas without using the short cut of a certain vocabulary – otherwise the end result would be both long-winded and a little patronising.

Secondly, when you're quoting writers like Herbert Marcuse or Karl Jaspers it would be strange if the surrounding text was in a completely different register – the flow wouldn't be there. Thirdly, part of the theme of *The Anarchist Revelation* is criticising the lowering of the intellectual level of today's society and the denial by the narrow positivist mindset of people's ability to think clearly and profoundly. Dumbing-down the language in which that sort of argument is expressed seems to me like something of an own goal!

It's not just a question of vocabulary, but also the way

ideas are expressed. Everything doesn't always have to be compressed into soundbites. I do take on board the criticism to a certain extent, though, and I would like to work on ways of communicating these ideas in a way that they can be more readily absorbed.

Q: Finally, your book draws on the work of a whole range of writers, many of whom are not anarchists. How would you respond to criticism that you risk diluting the anarchist message and confusing it with unrelated strands of thought. Is this some kind of "post-anarchism" that you're serving up?

No, it's not "post-anarchism". If anything, I'm trying to unearth an "Ur-anarchism", a primal force behind the philosophy, hence my foray into the worlds of hermeticism, alchemy, Sufism and Taoism. I think it's a mistake to imagine that anarchism is, or should be, some kind of self-contained bubble of consciously-limited political analysis. It's not airtight, but porous. Anarchism influences the world around it and it is, in turn, influenced by that world. The fact that an idea is expressed by a particular individual does not make it "their" idea anyway; it's all drawn from the common cultural resource of humanity.

So if a writer expresses something that seems valid and interesting to me, I don't have to agree with everything else they ever wrote or did in order for me to make use of it in my work and acknowledge where I read it. To me, it's actually exciting to find anarchist ideas bubbling up in unexpected places, as it makes it clear that our vision is not as peripheral as the thought-authorities would like to make out.

Anarchism is the political label we give to a massive underground river of suppressed thinking that is flowing under the streets of our materialist capitalist civilization, waiting to rise up and sweep away its factories, prisons and city halls. Ultimately, it's the life-force itself and as such it's unstoppable.

DON'T KILL YOURSELF!
A LETTER TO AN ANARCHIST FRIEND

I was deeply shocked by what you told me last night in the café. I know I didn't say much at the time, almost brushed it aside with a few empathetic mumblings.

But this morning I've been struck by the immense sadness behind your words and feel the need for a somewhat delayed reaction. You said, as I am sure you recall, that the world we live in is so bad, so far beyond redemption, that you feel like killing yourself to escape from it.

I never would have imagined that you could feel like that – feel like I do, in fact, though I'll come back to that later.

You are, after all, young (from my point of view at least), perfectly healthy (apart from a slight cold which I am sure was not a pertinent factor!), in a stable and loving relationship, financially secure thanks to a job you don't seem to mind too much, actively involved in trying to make the world a better place...

I suppose I shouldn't be surprised that this is not enough. Why should it be? But you've always seemed to me like someone blessed with an inner force of positivity, propelling you forward with such momentum as to leave doubt and despair trailing helplessly along behind.

Maybe if your life had stopped in some way, then I would

have accepted that all this debris had caught you up and entangled you in its confusion.

But then it's not really about you at all, is it? Any more than my own unease and anxiety are about me and my little life.

You've had your eyes open long enough to see the whole picture, the picture that most people around us have to blank out of their consciousnesses in order to remain "sane" – which means to carry on living out their phoney existences in a phoney manner without being troubled by the inconvenience of thought.

You've seen all that. You've seen the layers upon layers of lies that smother us and stop us from growing tall and strong inside as nature intended.

You've clambered up on the shoulders of the people you've met, the writers you've read, the dreams you've dreamt, and you've seen that beyond the wall that surrounds our everyday lives is another wall, and then another, in concentric circles marking out the limits of our identity, our freedom, our imagination, our potential.

We are all prisoners of a society, a civilization, so life-destroying, so corrupt, so ruthless, so brutal, so all encompassing, that all who see its hideous face revealed are in danger of being turned to stone – immobilised by the sickening dread of complete powerlessness.

How can we destroy this monstrous machine that is pulping into mincemeat so many tender, hopeful, human beings like you?

How can we even start the task of destroying it? Or think about starting to do so?

Whose life is long enough, whose energy and courage sufficient, whose patience and perseverance so divine that they could embark upon such a mission with any kind of confidence?

How can you free someone who doesn't even know they are a slave? How can you inspire people to win back something they don't even realise they've lost?

How can you urge them on to fight an enemy that they can't see, that they can't distinguish from the wobbly stage scenery and cardboard props of what they have been taught to think of as reality?

After generation upon generation in cages, do birds lose the urge to fly? Or do they just accept that a feeble fluttering from perch to perch is the nearest they are ever going to get?

No, it's not enough, this half-life we are condemned to lead, with chains and blinkers on our souls as we trudge on and on, turning the treadmill of profit for the greedy, loathsome few, sometimes holding hands or singing together to make us feel less worthless. It's not enough even to have tried to escape, to have smashed your head against the wall time and time again, the blood mixing with your tears as you scream that you WILL be free.

And it's not enough to find some quiet corner of the global prison where you can pretend you are at liberty, to crouch in some sheltered spot, behind a bush maybe, and hum sweet songs to yourself with fingers firmly planted in both ears to stop the sound of humanity's wailing from disturbing your reverie.

It's not enough, I know, and I have also often thought that suicide was the only way out – a comforting emergency exit in case it all does finally become unbearable.

My own contemplation of self-murder does not shock or thrill me any more, though. It bores me. It's been aired so often over the years, the decades in fact, that it's become stale and indigestible. But when you come out with same idea, it makes we want to weep.

Don't do it! Don't kill yourself! I don't know how serious you were, but don't even talk about it, let alone think about it!

I wouldn't say this if you were already dead, if you had sunk into a way of being so superficial that there really was no point in you staying alive, if you were compromised, polluted or stymied to such an extent that the earthly form we know as "you" had nothing left to offer.

I have nothing against suicide in some, nay many, circumstances. But to kill ourselves because of our despair at finding ourselves born and trapped in this prison-world is to miss out on an amazing opportunity.

When I was much younger, I had a vision of myself on the top floor of a multi-storey car park in the suburban town where I grew up.

I could no longer bear living in the realm of the plastic undead and I stood on the edge of the wall, the sun in my hair and the breeze making me squint, ready to step into the void.

At the very moment that I stepped out, an old man appeared from nowhere and pulled me back. I didn't know who he was at the time, but I suspect now that he was maybe the concept of my older self.

He told me that, instead of jumping from the car park, I should simply close my eyes and imagine I was doing so, imagine the fast falling, the impact, the end. I should think about everything that was now gone. My memories, my connections, my fears, my hopes, my perceived obligations.

And then, he said in this vision of mine, I should open my eyes again and find, to my astonishment, that I was still alive, still there, still real.

But all the rest of me had really gone. All those things I should or would have done would now never be accomplished. All that life I should or would have led would now never unfold. Nothing was expected of me. Nothing was demanded of me. I simply was.

Think now, he said, how and who you want to be, all freed from the burdens you have been persuaded to take upon yourself. Think now of what potential you possess as a raw human being with the power of moving, talking, interacting with the world around you.

You are an angel fallen from the sky, he said, still draped

in the afterbirth of the celestial mother. You have been sent here to do what you can, do what you must, to help bring about the great insurrection of the enslaved and dispossessed, to help crack open the crust of earthly power and deceit and unleash the tide of cleansing fire that swells beneath.

Imagine if all the would-be suicides in the world did the same – pulled back from the brink and became what they knew deep down they needed to be! What an army that would make, taking on the life-deniers with nothing left to lose!

He saw that I had understood and he said: "Just think – if you had really stepped over that edge, you would have died. Instead, you've been born".

I've always remembered this whenever I contemplate suicide, even though it only ever took place in my imagination. I like to think I have lived by it to some extent – but, I'm afraid, not as deeply as I would have liked.

It wasn't a one-off, though, and from time to time I leap again in my imagination, eyes tightly closed, and open them to find myself wrapped in a fresh skin, pulsating with new determination to leave my constructed self behind and throw my earthly presence, all clean and unencumbered, up against the scaly flesh of the Beast.

So don't kill yourself – just offer yourself up, time and time again to be used as they see fit by the forces of good, of life, of resistance to evil.

We are all lonely sparks of light, separated from the Whole and homesick for reunion.

That day will come soon enough, but while we still have our own separate form, we have work to do, a destiny to fulfil.

Long may you continue to shine!

ENDNOTES

ANTIBODIES

1. Herman Hesse, *Siddharta* (London: Picador, 1973) p. 114.
2. Eugène N Marais, *The Soul of the White Ant*, (London: Jonathan Cape, 1971) p. 16.
3. Marais, p. 67.
4. Marais, p. 67.
5. Marais, p. 52.
6. Rupert Sheldrake, *Dogs That Know When Their Owners Are Coming Home and other unexplained powers of animals*, (London: Arrow Books, 2000) p. 12.
7. Peter Kropotkin, *Mutual Aid: A Factor of Evolution*, (London: Freedom Press, 1993) p. 57.
8. Kropotkin, p. 51.
9. Kropotkin, p. 73.
10. Kit Pedler, *The Quest for Gaia: A Book of Changes*, (London: Granada, 1981) p. 163.
11. Kropotkin, p. 61.
12. Kropotkin, p. 129.
13. Kropotkin, p. 180.
14. Kropotkin, p. 84.
15. Kropotkin, pp. 84-85.
16. Kropotkin, p. 99.
17. Kropotkin, p. 52.
18. James Lovelock, *Gaia – A New Look at Life on Earth*, (Oxford: Oxford University Press, 2000) preface, x.
19. Lovelock, xii.
20. Pedler, p. 13.
21. Lovelock, p. 33.
22. Joseph Campbell, *The Masks of God: Oriental Mythology*, (London: Secker & Warburg, 1962) p. 4.
23. Peter Marshall, *Riding the Wind: A New Philosophy for a New Era*, (London: Continuum, 2000) p. 16.

24. Henry Margenau, *The Miracle of Existence*, (Boston and London: Shambhala, 1987) p. 106.

25. Campbell, p. 485.

26. Campbell, p. 494.

27. Campbell, pp. 12-14.

28. Campbell, p. 309.

29. *Meister Eckhart*, ed. by Halcyon Backhouse, (London: Hodder & Stoughton, 1992) p. 119.

30. *Meister Eckhart*, p. 49.

31. *Meister Eckhart*, pp. 122-123.

32. Roger Scruton, *Spinoza: A Very Short Introduction*, (Oxford: Oxford University Press, 2002) p. 35.

33. Scruton, p. 24.

34. Charles B Maurer, *Call to Revolution. The Mystical Anarchism of Gustav Landauer*, (Detroit: Wayne State University Press, 1971) p. 69.

35. Gustav Landauer, *Skepsis und Mystik: Versuche im Anschluss an Mauthners Sprachkritik*, (Cologne: 2d ed, 1923), p. 7, cit. Maurer, p. 69.

36. Landauer, *Skepsis und Mystik*, p. 10, cit. Maurer, p. 68.

37. Landauer, *Skepsis und Mystik*, p. 9, cit. Maurer, p. 68.

38. Landauer, *Die Revolution, vol 13, Die Gesellschaft*, ed. by Martin Buber, (Frankfurt: 1907), p. 20, cit. Maurer, p. 88.

39. Richard Jefferies, *The Story of My Heart: My Autobiography*, (London: Quartet, 1979) p. 56.

40. Marshall, p. 8.

41. Marshall, p. 19.

42. Eckhart Tolle, *A New Earth. Awakening to your life's purpose*, (London: Penguin, 2006) pp. 3-4.

43. Tolle, p. 276.

44. Scruton, pp. 53-54.

45. Scruton, p. 56.

46. Margenau, p. 33.

47. David Lorimer, *Whole in One. The Near-Death Experience and the Ethic of Interconnectedness*, (London: Arkana, 1990) p. 90.

48. Rupert Sheldrake, *The Sense of Being Stared At and other aspects of the extended mind*, (London: Arrow Books, 2004) p. 271.

49. Scruton, p. 37.

50. *Meister Eckhart*, p. 119.

51. CJ Jung, *Symbols of Transformation*, (New Jersey: Princeton University Press, 1967) p. 177, Two, IV, 259.

52. Pedler, p. 219.

53. Pedler, pp. 39-40.

54. Margenau, p. 120.

55. Landauer, *Skepsis und Mystik*, p. 13, cit. Maurer p. 71.

56. Campbell, p. 427.

57. Meister Eckhart, p. 78.

58. Maurer, p. 63.

59. Maurer, p. 71.

60. Pedler, p. 198.

61. Tolle, p. 268.

62. Jefferies, p. 49.
63. Jung, p. 202. Two, IV, 296.
64. Leo Tolstoy, *Life*, (London: Walter Scott, undated edition) p. 213.
65. Tolstoy, p. 37.
66. Tolle, pp. 56-57.
67. Jung, pp. 355-356. Two, VII, 553.
68. Pedler, p. 220.
69. Pedler, p. 68.
70. John Zerzan, *Running on Emptiness: The Pathology of Civilization*, (Los Angeles, Feral House, 2002) p. 78.
71. The Invisible Committee, *The Coming Insurrection*. (http://tarnac9.wordpress.com/texts/the-coming-insurrection, 2007) p. 20.
72. Maurer, pp. 108-109.
73. John Zerzan, *Future Primitive and Other Essays*, (Camberley: Green Anarchist Books, 1996) p. 145.
74. Maurer, pp. 90-91.
75. Kropotkin, p. 154.
76. Kropotkin, pp. 161-62.
77. Kropotkin, p. 178.
78. Kropotkin, p. 183.
79. Kropotkin, p. 76.
80. Kropotkin, p. 105.
81. Campbell, p. 10.
82. Campbell, p. 32.
83. Campbell, pp. 93-94.
84. Campbell, p. 112.
85. Zerzan, *Running*, p. 13.
86. Zerzan, *Future*, pp. 18-19.
87. Jung, p. 86. One, V, 129.
88. Zerzan, *Running*, p. 4.
89. Zerzan, *Running*, p. 6.
90. Zerzan, *Running*, p. 16.
91. Zerzan, *Running*, p. 10.
92. Tolle, p. 37.
93. Tolle, p. 128.
94. Tolle, p. 54.
95. Kropotkin, p. 105.
96. Invisible Committee, p. 23.
97. Landauer, *Aufruf zum Sozialismus*, (Berlin: 2nd ed, 1919) pp. 19-20, cit. Maurer, p. 93.
98. Landauer, *Sind das Ketzergedanken?*, in *Von Judentum: Ein Sammelbuch herausgegeben vom verein Jüdischer Hochschüler Bar Kochba in Prag*, ed. by Hans Kohn, (Prague: 1913) p. 252, cit. Maurer, p. 81.
99. Landauer, *Briefe, I*, p. 430, cit. Maurer, p. 79.
100. Pedler, p. 192.
101. Tolle, p. 122.
102. Marshall, p. 31.
103. Landauer, *Die Revolution*, p. 40, cit. Maurer, p. 89.
104. Jung, p. 178, Two, IV, 259.

105. Marais, p. 15.
106. Sheldrake, *Dogs*, p. 129.
107. Sheldrake, *Dogs*, p. 12.
108. Edward Selous, *Thought Transference or What?* in *Birds*, (London: Constable, 1931) p. 10, cit. Sheldrake, *Dogs*, p. 131.
109. Sheldrake, *Dogs*, p. 158.
110. Sheldrake, *Dogs*, p. 159.
111. Sheldrake, *Dogs*, p. 166.
112. Sheldrake, *Dogs*, pp. 264-65.
113. Sheldrake, *Dogs*, p. 266.
114. Zerzan, *Running*, p. 22.
115. Sheldrake, *The Sense*, p. 283.
116. Lorimer, p. 40.
117. Lorimer, p. 267.
118. Lorimer, p. 22.
119. *Meister Eckhart*, pp. 17-18.
120. Tolle, pp. 218-19.
121. Jefferies, p. 57.
122. Jefferies, p. 33.
123. Jefferies, p. 133.
124. Campbell, p. 114.
123. Marshall, p. 17.
126. Maurer, pp. 140-41.
127. Landauer, *Aufruf*, pp. 6-7, cit. Maurer p. 121.
128. Landauer, *Aufruf*, p. 34, cit. Maurer, p. 118.
129. Landauer, *Skepsis*, pp. 7-8, cit. Maurer, p. 68.
130. Albert Camus, *Resistance, Rebellion and Death*, (London: Hamish Hamilton, 1964) pp. 195-96.
131. Camus, p. 187.
132. Kropotkin, p. 231.
133. Camus, p. 77.
134. Pedler, p. 57.
135. Lovelock, p. 21.
136. Marais, p. 43.
137. Lovelock, p. 139.
138. Marais, pp. 44-45.
139. Lovelock, p. 26.
140. Lovelock, p. 29.
141. Lovelock, p. 29.
142. Pedler, p. 19.
143. Pedler, p. 161.
144. Campbell, p. 436.
145. Zerzan, *Running*, pp. 80-81.
146. Derrick Jensen, *Endgame – Volume 1, The Problem of Civilization*, (New York: Seven Stories Press, 2006) p. 75.
147. Pedler, p. 190.
148. Jung, p. 292, Two, VI, 447.
149. Tolstoy, p. 273.
150. Lorimer, p. 262, discussing work of David Bohm.

151. Camus, pp. 29-30.
152. Tolstoy, p. 141.
153. *Spinoza's Ethics 4, Appendix*, cit. Scruton, p. 91.
154. Lao Tzu, *Tao Te Ching*, (Harmondsworth: Penguin, 1963) pp. 111-13.
155. Kropotkin, p. 218.
156. Meister Eckhart, p. 135.
157. Maurer, p. 133.
158. Landauer, *Aufruf*, xvii, cit. Maurer p. 189.
159. Invisible Committee, p. 6, preface, dated January 2009.
160. Landauer, *Beginnen: Aufsätze über Sozialismus*, ed. by Martin Buber, Cologne, 1924, p. 16, cit. Maurer, p. 92.
161. Zerzan, *Future*, p. 130.
162. Jung, p. 398, Two, VIII, 617.
163. Zerzan, *Running*, p. 89.

BIOGRAPHICAL NOTES

Joseph CAMPBELL (1904-1987) was an American author and expert in comparative mythology and comparative religion. The works of German philosophers Arthur Schopenhauer and Friedrich Nietzsche had a profound effect on his thinking. Film director George Lucas has said Campbell's work inspired his 1977 sci-fi classic Star Wars.

Albert CAMUS (1913-1960) was a French Algerian author, philosopher, and journalist who was awarded the Nobel Prize for Literature in 1957. He was a key philosopher of the 20th-century and his most famous work is the novel *L'Étranger*. Often thought of as an existentialist, he in fact rejected that label and had serious differences with its leading proponent Jean-Paul Sartre. He died in a car crash at the age of 46.

Meister ECKHART (c. 1260-1328) was German theologian, philosopher and mystic Eckhart von Hochheim. Tried as a heretic by Pope John XXII, he apparently died before the verdict was declared, but no record of his death or burial has ever been discovered. His hand is often seen behind the influential 14th century anonymous *Theologia Germanica* which circulated after his disappearance.

The INVISIBLE COMMITTEE are an anonymous group of contributors who penned *The Coming Insurrection*, a booklet predicting the imminent collapse of capitalist culture, first published in 2007. In 2008 a group of French radicals, who became known as the Tarnac Nine, were arrested on charges of sabotaging high-speed railway lines, with the French state claiming they were the authors of the widely-distributed and influential pamphlet.

Richard JEFFERIES (1848-1887) was an English journalist and nature writer, noted for his depiction of English rural life, who also wrote *After London* (1885) an early work of post-apocalyptic science fiction. He struggled with poverty and tuberculosis and died in Goring, Sussex, at the age of 38.

Derrick JENSEN (born 1960) is an American author and environmental activist who has published several books questioning and critiquing contemporary society and its values, including *A Language Older Than Words, The Culture of Make Believe*, and *Endgame*.

Carl JUNG (1875-1961) was a celebrated Swiss psychiatrist, an influential thinker and the founder of analytical psychology. He also explored Eastern and Western philosophy, alchemy, astrology, sociology, as well as literature and the arts. He is perhaps best known for his theory of the collective unconscious.

Peter KROPOTKIN (1842-1921) was a Russian geographer, zoologist and anarchist. His many books, pamphlets and articles include *The Conquest of Bread* and *Fields, Factories and Workshops*, as well as *Mutual Aid: A Factor of Evolution*. He was also a contributor to the *Encyclopædia Britannica* Eleventh Edition.

LAO-TZU (c500BC) was an ancient Chinese philosopher and central figure in Taoism. He is traditionally regarded as the author of the *Tao Te Ching*, though this is often disputed and many insist he was not even a single person, but a collective designation for a school of thought represented by various historical figures, with his name meaning simply Old Master.

Gustav LANDAUER (1870-1919) was a leading German-Jewish anarchist theorist and is also known for his study and translations of William Shakespeare's works into German. Following the collapse of the 1918 Bavarian Revolution and the recapture of Munich by the German army and Freikorps units, Landauer was arrested and then stoned to death by soldiers in Stadelheim Prison.

David LORIMER is a contemporary Scottish writer, lecturer and editor who, after a career as a merchant banker, became a teacher of philosophy and modern languages at Winchester College in Hampshire. He has translated and edited books about the Bulgarian sage Peter Deunov and is a member of the International Futures Forum.

James LOVELOCK (born 1919) is an English scientist and author famed for proposing the Gaia theory. He has stirred controversy by openly supporting nuclear power, declaring in 2005: "I am a Green, and I entreat my friends in the movement to drop their wrongheaded objection to nuclear energy".

Eugène MARAIS (1871-1936) was a South African lawyer, naturalist, poet and writer. Embittered by the horrors of the Boer War, Marais refused to translate his works into English and as a result they remained almost unknown outside of southern Africa. A morphine addict and depressive, he committed suicide at the age of 65.

Henry MARGENAU (1901-1997) was a German-American physicist and philosopher who became Professor Emeritus of Physics and Natural Philosophy at Yale University. His scientific research included microwave theory and spectral line broadening and his written works include *The Nature of Physical Reality* and *The Miracle of Existence.*

Peter MARSHALL (born 1946) is an English philosopher, historian, biographer, travel writer and poet. He has written 15 books, translated into 14 different languages. Sussex-born Marshall has written on subjects including anarchism, ecology, alchemy and archaeology and has been described by *Resurgence* magazine as one of the 25 'visionary voices' who shaped the new world view in the last quarter of the 20th century.

Charles B MAURER published his biography of Gustav Landauer in 1971. At the time he was library director at Denison University, Granville, Ohio, USA. Educated at the University of Michigan and Northwestern University, he was a Woodrow Wilson Fellow at the University of Munich in 1960-61.

Fritz MAUTHNER (1849-1923) was a German-speaking Bohemian philosopher and writer and a major influence on Gustav Landauer. He is best known for his *Beiträge zu einer Kritik der Sprache*, which was published in three parts in 1901 and 1902.

Kit PEDLER (1927-1981) was an English scientist and author, who also penned science fiction and became the unofficial scientific adviser to the *Doctor Who* TV series in the 1960s, helping create the Cybermen as a warning of the threat posed by technology. He also co-wrote two series of *Doomwatch* for the BBC in the early 1970s.

Rupert SHELDRAKE (born 1942) is an English biochemist and plant physiologist who advances his own theory of morphic resonance and writes and researches on areas including animal and plant development and behaviour, memory, telepathy, perception and cognition in general.

Baruch de SPINOZA (1632-1677) was a Dutch philosopher of Portuguese Jewish origin, whose importance was not recognised until years after his death. Shunned by both Jewish and Roman Catholic establishments, he died at the age of 44 of a lung disease probably caused by fine glass dust from his trade as a lens grinder.

Eckhart TOLLE (born 1948) is a German-born author, public speaker and teacher on spirituality, who now lives in Canada. Originally Ulrich Leonard Tolle, he changed his forename to Eckhart because of his admiration for Meister Eckhart and left Germany after feeling depressed by the "pain in the energy field of the country", especially when playing in bombed-out buildings as a child.

Leo TOLSTOY (1828-1910), or Count Lev Nikolayevich Tolstoy, was a great Russian novelist and thinker, who wrote *War and Peace* and *Anna Karenina*, as well as novellas such as *The Death of Ivan Ilyich* and *The Kreutzer Sonata*. His views on non-violent resistance had a major influence on both Gandhi and Martin Luther King. He died of pneumonia at a railway station in 1910 after leaving home in the middle of winter at the age of 82.

John ZERZAN (born 1943) is an American anarchist and primitivist philosopher and author. His works criticize agricultural civilization and challenge domestication, language, symbolic thought and the concept of time. He has long been associated with *Green Anarchy*, a journal of anarcho-primitivist and insurrectionary anarchist thought.

ANARCHANGELS

1. Hermann Hesse, *Demian*, (London: Peter Owen, 2001) p. 181.
2. Gustav Landauer, *Revolution and Other Writings: A Political Reader*, ed. and trans. by Gabriel Kuhn (Oakland: PM Press, 2010) p. 74.
3. "To be fully at ease in a limited sphere, whatever it may be, one must be blind to the possibility of there being anything beyond". René Guénon, *East and West*, (Hillsdale NY: Sophia Perennis, 2001) p. 53.
4. Guénon defines progress as "a profound decadence, continuously accelerating, which is dragging humanity toward the pit where pure quantity reigns". René Guénon, *The Reign of Quantity and the Signs of the Times*, (Hillsdale NY: Sophia Perennis, 2004) p. 61.
5. "Just as an individual can be hostage in the abyss of addiction, so can an entire epoch or culture. This is true for our epoch, which is plunged into the World's Night. Western civilisation is experiencing a Dark Night of the Soul due to our self-asserting will to control, epitomized by the technology that we expect to provide us with a secure, happy and comfortable life". Linda Schierse Leonard, *Witness to the Fire, Creativity and the Veil of Addiction*, (Boston and London: Shambhala, 1990) p. 197.
6. "What the modern world has striven after with all its strength, even when it has claimed in its own way to pursue science, is really nothing other than the development of industry and machinery; and in thus seeking to dominate matter and bend it to their service, men have only succeeded, as we said at the beginning of this book, in becoming its slaves". René Guénon, *The Crisis of the Modern World*, (Ghent NY: Sophia Perennis, 2001) p. 87.
7. "Modern civilisation suffers from a lack of principles, and it suffers from it in every domain. By a monstrous anomaly, it is, alone, among the others, a civilization without principles, or with only negative ones, which amounts to the same thing. It is as if an organism with its head cut off went on living a life that was at the same time intense and disordered..." Guénon, *East and West*, p. 106.
8. "The great ability of those who are in control in the modern world lies in making the people believe that they are governing themselves". Guénon, *The*

Crisis of the Modern World, p. 74.

9. "All nationalism is essentially opposed to the traditional outlook". Guénon, *The Crisis of the Modern World*, p. 98

10. "What does the truth matter in a world whose aspirations, being solely material and sentimental and not intellectual, find complete satisfaction in industry and morality, two spheres where indeed one can very well do without conceiving the truth?" Guénon, *East and West*, p. 13.

11. Landauer famously wrote: "The state is a social relationship; a certain way of people relating to one another. It can be destroyed by creating new social relationships; ie, by people relating to one another differently". (Landauer, epigraph) But his views were more complex than might be realised by a superficial reading of this comment (*see 13*).

12. "The belief in indefinite progress is, all told, nothing more than the most ingenuous and the grossest of all kinds of 'optimism'; whatever forms this belief may take, it is always sentimental in essence, even when it is concerned with 'material progress'. If it be objected that we ourselves have recognized the existence of this progress, we reply that we have only done so as far as the facts warrant, which does not in the least imply an admission that it should, or even that it can, continue its course indefinitely; furthermore, as we are far from thinking it the best thing in the world, instead of calling it progress we would rather call it quite simply development; it is not in itself that the word progress offends us, but because of the idea of 'value' that has come almost invariably to be attached to it". Guénon, *East and West*, pp. 23-24.

"The materialists, with all their boasted 'good sense' and all the 'progress' of which they proudly consider themselves to be the most finished products and the most 'advanced' representatives, are really only beings in whom certain faculties have become atrophied to the extent of being completely abolished". Guénon, *The Reign of Quantity and the Signs of the Times*, p. 106.

13. "During the time of revolution, those men are the greatest who most decidedly and effectively negate". Landauer, p. 150.

14. "According to all the indications furnished by the traditional doctrines, we have in fact entered upon the last phase of the Kali-Yuga, the darkest period of this 'dark age', the state of dissolution from which it is impossible to emerge other than by a cataclysm, since it is not a mere readjustment that is necessary at such a stage, but a complete renovation". Guénon, *The Crisis of the Modern World*, p. 17.

Joseph Campbell describes the Jains' vision of a similar dark age: "The days will be hot, the nights cold, disease will be rampant and chastity nonexistent. Tempests will sweep over the earth and toward the conclusion of the period these will increase. In the end all life, human and animal, and all the vegetable seeds, will be forced to seek shelter in the Ganges, in miserable caves, and in the sea". Joseph Campbell, *The Hero With a Thousand Faces*, (London: Fontana Press, 1993) p. 264.

15. "The increase in the speed of events, as the end of the cycle draws near, can be compared to the acceleration that takes place in the fall of heavy bodies: the course of the development of the present humanity closely resembles the movement of a mobile body running down a slope and going faster as it approaches the bottom". Guénon, *The Reign of Quantity and the*

Signs of the Times, p. 43.

16. "The course of the manifested world toward its substantial pole ends at last in a 'reversal', which brings it back, by an instantaneous transmutation, to its essential pole; and it may be added that, in view of this instantaneity, and contrary to certain erroneous conceptions of the cyclical movement, there can be no 'reascent' of an exterior order following the 'descent', the course of manifestation as such being always descending from the beginning to the end". Guénon, *The Reign of Quantity and the Signs of the Times*, p. 163 (footnote).

17. "Man is not restricted at any stage to the passive role of a mere spectator, who must confine himself to forming an idea more or less true, or more or less false, of what is happening around him; on the contrary, he is himself one of the factors that intervene actively in the modification of the world he lives in; and it must be added that he is even a particularly important factor, by reason of the characteristically 'central' position he occupies in that world". Guénon, *The Reign of Quantity and the Signs of the Times*, p. 116.

18. See *Antibodies*.

19. Without fear. A slogan of the 2011 attempted "Spanish Revolution", inspired by the Arab Spring of the same year.

20. "This is the destiny of revolution in our times: to provide a spiritual pool for humanity. It is in revolution's fire, in its enthusiasm, its brotherhood, its aggressiveness that the image and the feeling of positive unification awakens; a unification that comes through a connecting quality: love as force". Landauer, p. 170.

21. "The modern hero, the modern individual who dares to heed the call and seek the mansion of that presence with whom it is our whole destiny to be atoned, cannot, indeed must not, wait for his community to cast off its slough of pride, fear, rationalized avarice, and sanctified misunderstanding. 'Live,' Nietzsche says, "as though the day were here.' It is not society that is to guide and save the creative hero, but precisely the reverse. And so every one of us shares the supreme ordeal – carries the cross of the redeemer – not in the bright moments of his tribe's great victories, but in the silences of his personal despair". Campbell, p. 391.

22. "In order for a fundamental turn to take place in our time, in order for a spiritual transformation to occur, there must be those who venture into The Abyss and encounter it... The ground must be prepared for the divine radiance to shine and be seen". Paraphrasing of Heidegger by Schierse Leonard, p. 199.

"He is resolved to forget that the desperate clinging to the self and the desperate clinging to life are the surest way to eternal death, while the power to die, to strip one's self naked, and the eternal surrender of the self bring immortality with them". Hermann Hesse, *Steppenwolf*, (London: Penguin, 2011) p. 76.

23. Stephan A Hoeller writes of the need for a new kind of human being, neither a "consumer-robot" nor an "outdated Marxist image of the proletarian revolutionary who naively believes that the basic evils of human nature can be solved by political force and economic change. Rather, the new man and woman must be Abraxas: with head overshadowed by the Logos of wisdom and insight, with swift feet that possess the instinctual force and libidinal

resilience of the serpent. Those opposites in turn must be joined and welded together by qualities of true and undisguised humanity, a humanity for which no moral, economic or political apologies are required". Stephan A Hoeller, *The Gnostic Jung and the Seven Sermons to the Dead*, (Wheaton IL: Quest, 1994) p. 175.

24. "We do not intend to flee from the *vita activa* to the *vita contemplativa*, nor vice versa, but to keep moving forward while alternating between the two, being at home in both, partaking of both". Hermann Hesse, *The Glass Bead Game*, (London: Vintage Books, 2000) p. 223.

25. "Isolated societies, dream-bounded within a mythologically charged horizon, no longer exist except as areas to be exploited. And within the progressive societies themselves, every last vestige of the ancient human heritage of ritual, morality, and art is in full decay". Campbell, pp. 387-88.

26. "True history might endanger certain political interests; and it may be wondered if this is not the reason, where education is concerned, why certain methods are officially imposed to the exclusion of all others; consciously or not, they begin by removing everything that might make it possible to see things clearly, and that is how 'public opinion' is formed". Guénon, *East and West*, p. 15.

27. Warns Hoeller: "The 'new age' optimism and superficiality of those who reduce the dark mysteries of Jung's Gnosis to the shallow level of their own limitations are apt to make people into the victims of the very unconscious they tend to treat so lightly". Hoeller, p. 203.

28. "Let there be no confusion on this point: if the general public accepts the pretext of 'civilization' in all good faith, there are those for whom it is no more than mere moralistic hypocrisy, serving as a mask for designs of conquest or economic ambitions. It is really an extraordinary epoch in which so many men can be made to believe that a people is being given happiness by being reduced to subjection, by being robbed of all that is most precious to it, that is to say of its own civilisation, by being forced to adopt manners and institutions that were made for a different race, and by being constrained to the most distasteful kinds of work, in order to make it acquire things for which it has not the slightest use. For that is what is taking place: the modern West cannot tolerate that men should prefer to work less and be content to live on little; as it is only quantity that counts, and as everything that escapes the senses is held to be non-existent, it is taken for granted that anyone who is not in a state of agitation and who does not produce much in a material way must be 'lazy'". Guénon, *The Crisis of the Modern World*, p. 92.

29. "It would not be too much to say that myth is the secret opening through which the inexhaustible energies of the cosmos pour into human cultural manifestation. Religions, philosophies, arts, the social forms of primitive and historic man, prime discoveries in science and technology, the very dreams that blister sleep, boil up from the basic, magic ring of myth". Campbell, p. 3. "It has always been the prime function of mythology and rite to supply the symbols that carry the human spirit forward, in counteraction to those other constant human fantasies that tend to tie it back. In fact, it may well be that the very high incidence of neuroticism among ourselves follows from the decline among us of such effective spiritual aid". Campbell, p. 11. "For they actually touch and bring into play the vital energies of the whole

human psyche. They link the unconscious to the fields of practical action, not irrationally, in the manner of a neurotic projection, but in such fashion as to permit a mature and sobering, practical comprehension of the fact-world to play back, as a stern control, into the realms of infantile wish and fear. And if this be true of the comparatively simple folk mythologies (the systems of myth and ritual by which the primitive hunting and fishing tribes support themselves), what may we say of such magnificent cosmic metaphors as those reflected in the great Homeric epics, the Divine Comedy of Dante, the Book of Genesis, and the timeless temples of the Orient? Until the most recent decades, these were the support of all human life and the inspiration of philosophy, poetry, and the arts. Where the inherited symbols have been touched by a Lao-tse, Buddha, Zoroaster, Christ or Mohammed – employed by a consummate master of spirit as a vehicle of the profoundest moral and metaphysical instruction – obviously we are in the presence rather of immense consciousness than of darkness. And so, to grasp the full value of the mythological figures that have come down to us, we must understand that they are not only symptoms of the unconscious (as indeed are all human thoughts and acts) but also controlled and intended statements of certain spiritual principles, which have remained as constant throughout the course of human history as the form and nervous structure of the human physique itself". Campbell, p. 257.

30. "The effect of the successful adventure is the unlocking and release again of the flow of life into the body of the world". Campbell, p. 40.

THE POLITICS OF FEAR

The important 1992 Timewatch documentary on Gladio can be found online on YouTube – at the time of writing, go to:
http://www.youtube.com/watch?v=trGfQREzScY
Daniele Ganser, *Nato's Secret Armies: Operation Gladio and Terrorism in Western Europe* (London: Cass, 2005)
Philip Willan, *Puppet Masters – The Political Use of Terrorism in Italy* (London: Constable, 1991)
Stewart Angell, *The Sussex Secret Resistance* (Midhurst: Middleton Press, 1996)
William Mackenzie, *The Secret History of SOE – Special Operations Executive 1940-1945* (London: St Ermin's Press, 2000)
Martin Ingram & Greg Harkin, *Stakeknife – Britain's Secret Agents in Ireland* (Dublin: O'Brien Press, 2004)
John Pilger, *The New Rulers of the World* (London: Verso, 2002)
Noam Chomsky, *The Culture of Terrorism* (London: Pluto, 1988)
Naomi Klein, *The Shock Doctrine – The Rise of Disaster Capitalism* (London: Allen Lane, 2007)
Guardian report on Gladio
http://www.cambridgeclarion.org/press_cuttings/gladio_graun_5dec1990.html

Reichstag fire
http://en.wikipedia.org/wiki/Reichstag_fire
Bologna bombing
http://en.wikipedia.org/wiki/Bologna_bombing
Bologna bombing – 25 years on
http://www.threemonkeysonline.com/a-massacre-to-remember-the-bologna-train-station-bombing-twenty-five-years-later/
P2
http://en.wikipedia.org/wiki/Propaganda_Due
Moro
http://en.wikipedia.org/wiki/Aldo_Moro#cite_note-R89-13
Fascinating 85-minute interview on Gladio and related issues with author Daniele Ganser
http://www.youtube.com/watch?v=8SeM7lDCFCc
Report – German intelligence link to neo-Nazi terrorists
http://www.guardian.co.uk/world/2011/nov/15/germany-neo-nazi-terror-cell-doner-killings
Report – FBI created "Islamic" terrorists
http://www.guardian.co.uk/world/2011/nov/16/fbi-entrapment-fake-terror-plots
Report – British intelligence link to IRA
http://www.guardian.co.uk/uk/2011/sep/11/ira-murders-claim-to-smithwick?INTCMP=ILCNETTXT3487
Report – Covert world of "counter-terrorism"
http://www.guardian.co.uk/world/2011/sep/11/smithwick-tribunal-ian-hurst-analysis
Video – Israelis train to Kurdish guerrillas
http://www.youtube.com/watch?v=2sX4XPNlEqE
Report – Israel link to PKK
http://www.todayszaman.com/news-257074-possible-consequences-of-pkk-israeli-unionby-othman-ali*.html
Report – Israel and the PKK
http://www.haaretz.com/news/diplomacy-defense/turkey-fm-condemns-israeli-plan-to-support-pkk-1.383801

LI AND ORGANIC ANARCHY

1. Alan Watts, *Tao: The Watercourse Way*, with the collaboration of Al Chung-Liang Huang (London, Arkana, 1992) p. 43.
2. Watts, p. 46.
3. Watts, p. 51.

TRANSCENDENT ANARCHY

1. June Singer, *Boundaries of the Soul: The Practice of Jung's Psychology* (New York: Anchor Books, 1989) p. 314.
2. Singer, p. 319.
3. Singer, p. 321.
4. Singer, p. 333.

ABOUT THE AUTHOR

Paul Cudenec is a writer, poet and activist living in the south of England. His recent writing includes *The Anarchist Revelation: Being What We're Meant To Be* (2013) also available from Winter Oak. For more information and contact details visit paulcudenec.blogspot.co.uk